How to Think Independently
Learn how to think, not what to think

Glenn Baloban

Copyright © 2019 by Glenn Baloban

All rights reserved. No part of this publication may be reproduced, distributed, or transmitted in any form or by any means, including photocopying, recording, or other electronic or mechanical methods, without the prior written permission of the publisher, except in the case of brief quotations embodied in critical reviews and certain other non-commercial uses permitted by copyright law. For permission requests, write to the publisher, addressed Glennbusinessx@gmail.com

ISBN: 9781092997591

This book is dedicated to those who are living a life they wish to change.

Thinking,
A dear friend who keeps me up at night.

Contents

Introduction	7
Chapter One : It Starts with a Belief	9
Chapter Two : The Education System	16
Chapter Three : Research and Self-education	21
Chapter Four : Dogmatism and Open-Mindedness	27
Chapter Five : How to Stand up for Yourself	33
Chapter Six : Toxic and Negative People	39
Chapter Seven : Relationships and Self-love	47
Chapter Eight : How to Find Your Life Purpose	54
Chapter Nine : Creating an Impactful Life Purpose	60
Chapter Ten : Down to Business	69
Chapter Eleven : Ideology and Remaining Independent	80
Chapter Twelve : Mindfulness and Social Media	87
Chapter Thirteen : Investing in Yourself	93
Chapter Fourteen : The Importance of Meditation	100
Conclusion	107
About the Author	111

Acknowledgements

Special thanks to everyone who made an important impact within my life:

Oliver Eclipse, Reinier Lann, Nettley Camilleri, Sue Killingbeck, Sarah Bonney, Jacinta Eve, Andre Simon, my parents, and my sister.

Introduction

Welcome to my humble book on how to think independently. To be successful in life, you must be *different*. The purpose of this book is to show you how to think independently, allowing you to rebel against conformity. I would like to start this book with a word of warning though. This book and my teachings can only take you as far as you allow them. In other words, you must remain open-minded, as dogmatism* will hinder your learning and ability to think independently. Also note that thinking independently is not an overnight accomplishment. Rather, it's a lifelong journey. My job is to prepare you for your journey by giving you the tools and ability to think for yourself. I won't teach you what to think, but *how* to think.

Within this book, I will share with you the meaning of life and teach you how to find your life's purpose. This will enable you to excel and succeed in your life. The benefits you will receive by thinking independently will be huge, especially compared to the people who remain ignorant and only think what they are told to think.

Thinking independently will give you access to:
- Never-ending growth
- Endless opportunities
- A meaningful life purpose

- Advanced knowledge
- Greater self-improvement
- Personal freedom
- Increased critical and strategic thinking
- See what others do not
- And most importantly, your own independence.

The reason I am so passionate about you thinking independently is because it's now your time to make a difference. The days of sitting in an office from 9–5 are ending. A new age stands before us, and it is an age of enlightenment*. It's time for the world to leave greed and corruption behind, and truly change our planet for the better. We live in a world where everyone is connected, which allows you and me to have a greater impact on the world. There is great power within you, and it's time for you to reach your full potential by stepping away from what you've been told and embracing independence. This book holds great wisdom and knowledge that will allow you to empower yourself.

Thinking independently is a super power that will allow you to see what others don't. So, as I teach you this super power, I encourage you to use it wisely, to benefit society, and help those in need. I encourage you to use the power of thinking independently to change the world for the better. Use it to feed the hungry, build houses for the homeless, save the environment, fight greed and corruption, and most importantly, ensure that generations to come have a safe place to call home. The time is now, not tomorrow. The present moment is all we have—and it's time to make a difference. Are you ready to make a difference?

Chapter One
It Starts with a Belief

We are born into this life not knowing a thing. We have no idea of how things work, what things look like, what is true, what is false, what is possible, and what is impossible. We are born completely innocent and open-minded, full of love and happiness. It is perfect enlightenment. But over time, this changes for most people. They become guilty, dogmatic, and lacking in love. Eventually, they lose their happiness.

It's as if something within us changes, taking away our happiness, but we can't quite put our finger on it. We start as a happy, joyful child, who is excited to wake up every day and explore this exciting, beautiful world, making friends along the way.

Yet over time, this begins to change. Instead, we work in miserable 9–5 jobs that we hate, and it becomes harder and harder to wake up in the morning and face our day. It becomes harder to make new friends. This world that was once exciting, beautiful, and full of amazing people and objects—instead becomes a world of money and benefits. We start to see the world as "How does this benefit me?" Or "How can I turn this into profit?" Or "How can I use this person to my advantage?"

Then at the end of each day, we ask ourselves "Why am I so unhappy with my life?" Or if we can't bear to face this question, we try to forget about it with booze, parties, TV, video games, social media, drugs, or some other distraction.

A sad truth about life, which I'm sure many of you already know, is that a lot of people don't end up living the life they dreamed of. If you ask a child "What do you want to be when you grow up?", most children will say they want to be an astronaut, a famous movie star, singer, or dancer. As a child, the sky is the limit, or just the beginning.

But instead, they finish school or college or university, and they find a job that they don't really like, but it pays a decent salary that helps them pay their college debt. Shortly after, they meet someone and get married. Then the newlywed couple are expecting their first child and have a house with a mortgage. Soon they're buried in day care and school fees, and eventually college fees again. So many people end up in this life—with no idea why.

Why do so many people start out with great ambitions and dreams in life, only to end up working in a job they hate or that has little meaning to them? The answer is due to the programming of society. I don't mean conspiracy theories here. I mean the broad philosophy of *get good grades, get a degree, find a good job, get married, buy a home, and have children.* A life plan that was taught to previous generations. This philosophy is often pushed on people in society, and those who are pushing it forget that it is merely a paradigm* among many, and an outdated one at that. Such a philosophy greatly benefits society; however, that doesn't mean it benefits you as an individual.

Before we continue, I would like to make something very clear. I am not attacking this lifestyle or philosophy, nor am I saying that it's insufficient in some way. Rather, I wish to make you more conscious of why people live such a lifestyle and how you can live a different lifestyle if you wish.

To do this, we must ask ourselves "How do people become indoctrinated* by the programming and conditioning* of society?" The answer to this question starts with **belief**. In my previous book *False Representations of Reality*, I go into great detail about how and why we hold beliefs. Here, I'll give you a brief overview that is relevant to this book.

Where beliefs come from

To begin, we must understand where a belief comes from and how it is formed. A belief comes from an idea, and the idea turns some form of chaos into order. In other words, a belief takes an unknown and turns it into a known—or turns some uncertainty into certainty. So, a belief comes from an idea that humans use to turn the unknown into known.

Whether that "known" or belief is correct is a completely different story. To give you an illustration of this, if I asked an atheist what happens when you die (death is the unknown), a common reply would be "There is nothingness, just unconsciousness, like before birth or a deep sleep." On the other hand, if I asked a Christian what happens when you die, they would tell me "There is an afterlife, and you either go to heaven or to hell." Both the atheist and the Christian are taking the unknown (death) and forming an idea out of that chaos. This idea eventually becomes a belief, which turns chaos into **order**. That is basically where a belief comes from and how it is formed.

Another very important thing to note is that the beliefs you hold determine your life and your perspective. Depending on the beliefs you have, this will impact the type of life that you experience. (I go into this subject in great detail in my other book in case you're interested). Now let's look at what determines the beliefs you accept and hold.

The role of culture

The major contributing factor in whether you believe something or not is your **culture**. Our culture brands us like livestock. Our culture determines the majority of our beliefs. For example, take Australia and America—both have very different cultures. In America, many citizens believe that the general public should have the right to own firearms. Whereas in Australia, the vast majority don't believe the general public should have this right. In American culture, guns are acceptable; however, in Australian culture, they are not acceptable. As you can see, the culture you grew up in strongly determines your perspective on firearms and whether you believe it's ethical for the public to own them or not.

Us humans are greatly impacted by our environment—or more accurately we are a result of our culture, because it is saturated in our environment. We are a product of our environment, because it determines our religious beliefs, the language we speak, our education, our ethics, the sports we enjoy, what we believe is fashionable, and what type of foods we eat. These factors contribute to our identity, and this is the reason why culture is so important to so many people.

What I'd like you to notice is that your culture gives you an identity—whether you like it or not. It's your culture that tells you who you are and what you represent, without you having a say about it (which is where a lot of stereotypes come from). Most people just accept the traditions and beliefs of their culture and live accordingly. In other words, why question what's already laid out for you?

By no means am I anti-culture in any way. I merely want you to understand where the majority of your beliefs come from. When you understand why you hold certain beliefs and where they come from, this gives you more power within your life. It allows you to think more freely and independently. You are powerful, and with the right tools to help you think independently, you can become unstoppable—with no limitations in life.

Exercise: Understand your beliefs

To understand this, I'd like to start with a mental exercise that I strongly encourage you to do. Sit down somewhere quiet, on your own, and be completely honest with yourself. Start to question why you hold certain beliefs and where they came from. Ask yourself "Why do I believe X, and where did my belief about X come from?" Eventually, you will find an answer to your questions within you. After you find an answer within yourself, once again question the answer you have just given yourself and ask "Why do I believe the answer I just gave myself is true"? For example:

Question: Why do I believe in God?
Answer: Because I believe in the Bible.

Question: Why do I believe in the Bible?
Answer: Because that's what people have told me to be true ever since I was a child.

Question: Why do people tell me that the Bible is true?
Answer: Because it is the word of God.

Question: What makes it the word of God?

The questions and answers go on and on, and eventually you'll come to a realization of why you believe what you believe. Your questions and answers are completely private—only you will know them. So don't be afraid to venture into the unknown or prove yourself wrong. Don't be afraid to give yourself answers that go against everything you believe, as this is where the most growth happens.

Pick a topic (it doesn't have to be about God) and question why you believe what you believe. Doing this mental exercise is the first step in independent thinking, as you will begin to discover why you believe in what you believe. If you want to think and be independent, you must have a deep understanding of yourself and who you are, which is what this book is all about and I will help you do exactly that.

A few topics and questions to get started with:

- How do I view money, and what does it mean to me?
- What are my beliefs about God?
- In what ways does my beliefs about God influence my thinking?
- Who am I?
- What are my ethics?
- What are my worldviews?
- What are my values, and why?
- What type of life do I want?
- Why do I live the type of life that I am living now?
- What areas of my life need fixing?
- Why can't I be honest with myself, or in what ways am I dishonest with myself?
- In what ways does my culture influence my thinking?

How to Think Independently

Be careful not to fall into a questioning paradox, where your answers and questions lead you in circles. If you find yourself doing this, it means either you're being dishonest with yourself or you need to expand your knowledge of the unknown. It's okay not to have an answer to a question. It's better to be honest and not have an answer, compared to creating a dishonest answer. How effective this exercise is completely depends on how much effort you're willing to put in and how honest you're willing to be with yourself. If you can't put in the effort or be honest with yourself, there is nothing I can teach you. If you're willing to put in the effort and be honest, then turn the page.

Chapter Two
The Education System

Now that you've started to question your beliefs and where they come from, you've put yourself ahead of most people. You're now more conscious and aware of why you believe the things you do. In fact, you may be surprised by the amount of people who don't know why they believe the things they do, and how many refuse to question it. But to remain dogmatic and ignorant is to be controlled by those who aren't. Unfortunately, there are many traps within society that both accidentally and deliberately take away your independent thinking, which I want to make you more aware of in this book.

The map is not the territory

The education system has a massive influence on your life and how you think. To be clear, I am not anti-education. I only wish to point out the influence and impact it has on your life. The education system takes you from a young age and slowly conditions and programs your behaviour. This consequently influences your beliefs—what you believe to be possible and true.

Not only has education become an outdated system, it also sets a lot of good people up for failure in life, because getting an A on an exam is not going to prepare you for the real world. What the education system fails to realise is that the map is not the territory—and mistaking the map for the territory is what causes many people to fail in life.

When I was in business class at night school, there were students who completed assignments and exams with outstanding results. However, when it came to implementing what they'd learnt in real life, they failed. That's not to say that my classmates didn't have the ability to run a business. Rather, business classes only prepared them to run a business on paper and not in real life. You see, just because something works in theory, that doesn't necessarily mean it will work in reality. That's why the map is not the territory.

My education experience

To put this into perspective, I'd like to share my personal experience in the education system as someone who has dyslexia. At the age of five, my teachers noticed that I was a bit different to the other kids, and not in a "special and gifted" way—more in a "he is slowing down the class" kind of way. They noticed that I had trouble with speech, writing, and reading. I would pronounce dish as "diss" or spell mother as "marfher", and had trouble reading basic sentences. After that, I began special education. I was often taken out of class, away from my peers, to practice my speech, spelling, and reading. When I wasn't in special ed, I had a substitute teacher in class who helped me and the other children who needed assistance. At the time, they believed I had a learning disability.

When I was nine, my mother took me to see a licensed educational psychologist, who gave me multiple tests on reading, writing, spelling, and puzzles. A few weeks after completing the tests, I was officially diagnosed with dyslexia and put on a "beat-dyslexia" course. I remember the psychologist telling me I had a chemical imbalance within my brain, which caused my learning disability —and that's why I couldn't read or write as well as the other children. At the time, I was crushed. I can still remember the sinking feeling in my chest as the psychologist explained how I was limited in my ability to learn and what this meant for my future.

Out of the 12 years that I was in school, I spent 10 of them attending special ed or needing assistance in class. I had to repeat year 11 math three times, as I continued to fail exams and assignments. I failed science with Ds and Es and scraped by in English with C minuses. And that only happened because my English teachers put in the extra effort to help me. If it wasn't for them, I would have failed English too. I completed year 12 but didn't pass, and therefore didn't have the grades to attend university. After school, I ended up working at the landfill or "the dump" as it's more commonly known.

When I left school, I felt so stupid and worthless—to the point where I believed my dyslexia was a curse. At 18, I hit rock bottom in life, because I didn't believe that I had a future. Then one day, I was messing around on YouTube, wasting time, and I stumbled across a Les Brown video. I clicked on it thinking he was a comedian. Instead, it was a motivation video, as Les Brown is a motivational speaker. During the speech, he talked about his disability and the struggles he went through, which I could closely relate to. Then he said a line that would change my life forever: "Someone's opinion of you does not have to become your reality."

Something within me changed that day—as if a spark ignited within me, making me more conscious of my life. Before I knew it, all I listened to was Les Brown tapes, and eventually I began to work out, which taught me many lessons in life. From that point onward, I began to spiral upwards, eventually outgrowing motivational types. My upwards spiral wasn't easy though, and there was a lot of suffering and many setbacks along the way. However, I made it.

Once I became more motivated, I started to educate myself, as I came to realise that the education system had taught me almost nothing. If anything, it had pushed limiting beliefs on me. After I started to self-educate, I quickly realised that I learnt perfectly fine. I watched education videos and spent time reading books and doing online courses. To my astonishment, I had a lot of fun and enjoyed learning, to the point where I'd spend up to 14 hours a day studying topics I was interested in! It was like my mind had been starving for all those years and was finally allowed to eat. Since then, my mind has greatly changed, and I think completely differently now.

The importance of self-education

This brings me to the next step in becoming independent and that is to **self-educate**. As you've no doubt seen, the education system has many flaws and errors, but realistically it's a very complex system to change, as it has become very political and that's why it's outdated. So instead of waiting for the education system to change, I encourage you to take the responsibility upon yourself to self-educate. Because in self-education, you get to learn what you want to learn, at the pace and style of your liking, and best of all there are no exams. For an added benefit, it's much cheaper compared to the traditional education system, especially with sites such as YouTube, Udemy, Skillshare, and Khan Academy that offer great educational services. Not to mention the countless books, eBooks, and audiobooks available on the topic of your choice.

Another important aspect of self-education is that it teaches you to research and find out whether something is true or not. In the traditional school system, you are just fed information from teachers and textbooks, and are mostly fed only one perspective, which often contains a lot of dogma. Self-education teaches you to do your own research, seek out the facts, and listen to multiple opinions and perspectives.

Now, looking back over my life, I realise that dyslexia is not a learning disability; rather it's a way of saying that the traditional educational system is not built for your learning style. Yes, if you're dyslexic like me, you may have trouble reading, spelling, writing, and speaking, but you must realise that these skills can be improved and worked on. It's very clear to me that dyslexia is not a learning disability. Saying to a child that dyslexia is a learning disability only sets them up with limiting beliefs, the kind that held me back for the first 18 years of my life. These days, I no longer see dyslexia as a curse or a disability; rather I see it as a gift that I am grateful for, as dyslexia enables me to see reality in the way that I do.

The education system has great limitations, but you do not. Therefore, if you wish to think independently, you must self-educate. We'll discuss how to self-educate through research in the next chapter.

Chapter Three
Research and Self-education

A foundational tool in independent thinking is **research**. If you wish to think independently, you must do your own research. What most people do when researching a topic is either read an article or watch a video, then use its conclusion as their own. You see this all the time in politics. People watch a bit of news, then they use that as evidence for why their political view is correct. This can become a problem when the source of information is incorrect, as people spread incorrect information around while they try to prove a point. In this chapter, we'll look at the importance of doing your own research on a topic.

Cherry-picking conclusions

A perfect illustration of this problem in action is the gender pay gap. Reports on the gender pay gap claim that women earn 79¢ on the dollar compared to men (close to that number depending on county). People then make the conclusion that companies are paying women less than men for the same work. Whether you believe this conclusion to be true is for you to decide. However, there is a lot that this figure doesn't tell you, which creates confusion for people who don't do their own research. The wage gap has a lot of complicated factors, such as working hours, children, occupation, experience, education, location, and choice. Due to the complexity of the problem, it is almost impossible to make a five-minute video or a 2000-word article to accurately explain why there is a wage gap, or more accurately an earnings gap, between men and women (in Western society) and how this impacts the economy.

This type of situation leads to lots of confusion when people only watch short news clips or YouTube videos or read something on Facebook. For this reason, I encourage you to research such topics for yourself (if you don't do this already). Because if you don't, then someone else is telling you how to think by giving you their conclusion.

Another illustration is religion and social media. Religious quotes are shared among users on social media platforms, which are used to defend and create new beliefs. Quotes such as "Fill your mind with God's word, and you will have no room for Satan's lies" or "If you lose everything but still have Jesus, you still have everything you need", and "Pray for those who don't have faith, as they know not what they do."

I've seen these quotes on Facebook pages that feature daily images and quotes about God. People share these quotes and use them in arguments to defend their beliefs. However, the problem with using such quotes as arguments is that people are cherry-picking information to push a religious agenda. This results in poorly-formed arguments that either don't make sense or end up going around in circles, such as just believing in God's word without question. I believe that religion makes some good points, such encouraging people to help the poor and unfortunate, and emphasising the importance of taking responsibility for oneself. However, these points become twisted and misleading if people fail to form good arguments and clarity around such teachings. With no clarity and a lack of research, religious teachings become dogmatic and dangerous.

To avoid such dogmatism and dangerous beliefs, it's important to learn how to correctly research heated and controversial topics such as religion and the earning gap between genders. Putting in the effort and work to self-research a topic can be long and burdensome, hence the reason why many people cherry-pick someone else's conclusion. However, if you wish to truly think for yourself, then you must put in the work to correctly research a topic and form an accurate and detailed perspective.

How to research a topic

Next, you will find some steps to research any topic, so you can form a strong argument, or more importantly find the truth.

1. Pick a topic.
2. Write a short argument on what you already believe to be correct, and what your opponent (if any) believes to be correct.
3. Determine what you're trying to solve or would like to know.
4. Gather as much information and data on the topic as you can (from multiple sources). Simple observation is an extremely powerful tool when gathering information.
5. Try to disprove your own argument. You can do this by listening to opposing views.
6. Create your own conclusion through deep contemplation.
7. Get feedback on your conclusion by asking other people questions or presenting your perspective. This enables you to continually improve your conclusion.

Here's an example of this for illustration (please note, this is not my actual opinion).

1. Abortion
2. I believe in pro-choice and believe people have the right to choose.
3. I would like to know why people oppose this view.
4. To research, I will read books, watch online videos, and listen to other people's opinions. This can be done by listening to the radio or podcasts. Other information I will gather is statistics on abortion from different countries and the process of abortion.
5. Using the newly-found information, I will form an argument for why abortion is wrong and why people should not be allowed to choose.
6. After this, I will form my new conclusion.
7. Finally, I will present my conclusion to other people to challenge what I believe and the information that I have gathered. I will adjust my conclusion if needed.

Your argument or perspective should be clear and easy to understand. If it is neither clear nor easy to understand, this is a sign that it's a poorly developed argument or perspective.

Direct experience is key

A large part of research is self-experimentation (experimenting for yourself) to directly experience the results. When it comes to research, **direct experience** is king; otherwise it's just hearsay. For example, empiricism is a theory that states that knowledge comes only or primarily from our five basic senses. If we did not have our five basic senses, we would not have knowledge. This is because consciousness is first order while awareness is second order. Meaning you can have consciousness without awareness however, you can't have awareness without consciousness. Our mind requires awareness to collect data, forming a memory.

Direct experience is anything that is directly in the present moment. Anything that is not in your direct experience is just concept and imagination. A good exercise to practice comprehending concept and imagination that I learnt from a monk is to put your hand in front of your face, so you're directly experiencing your hand. Then hide your hand behind your back so it's out of sight, and imagine what your hand looks like. When your hand is directly in front of you, it is actuality; the moment you place it behind your back, it becomes concept and imagination. This applies to everything. If it's not in your direct experience, then it just becomes concept and imagination.

When researching, it's important to be radically open-minded to get the best results. What I mean by radical open-mindedness is being open to new and strange ideas. However, it does not mean that you just accept and believe these ideas without direct proof. For example, if I was researching telekinesis, I would be open to the idea that it could be a real thing and possible. However, I wouldn't just accept and believe it was possible based off hearsay or a YouTube video. For me to believe in telekinesis, I would have to self-experiment or directly experience it from someone else. I encourage you be as open-minded as possible to new ideas and beliefs, even though they may sound strange or controversial at first. If you're able to remain open-minded, you'll be surprised at what you would have missed otherwise.

Once you have become open-minded about a topic, the key to quality research is **observation**. Observation is the most powerful tool you can use when researching. For example, if you want to learn about the nature of bees, the best method is not Googling "bees", but rather going outside and observing bees within your garden. Watch what they do and how they do it. The longer you observe the bees going about their day, the more you will learn. Eventually, you'll be able to tell the difference between bee species, and you'll know what flowers bees like best, the time of day that bees are most active, and how many bees there are in one garden.

If you wish to truly understand anything in life, you can't just listen to someone else's opinions and conclusions, then repackage it as your own. Instead, you must observe and do your own research, which will take time and effort. That is the only way. I understand that this may be a disappointing answer to some, yet from my perspective it is nothing more than the truth. Therefore, I encourage you to research and find out for yourself, to see whether my truth is your truth. Remember, it's also important that you don't just believe everything I say—instead question what I say. Only by questioning those who teach you will you ever learn from your teachers. In the next chapter, we'll discuss dogmatism and open-mindedness, which will allow you to ask deeper questions.

Chapter Four
Dogmatism and Open-Mindedness

To close your mind is to close the door on new experiences. So far, I've briefly mentioned dogmatism and the importance of open-mindedness. In this chapter, I'll go into more detail. Because if you want to think independently and be the best version of yourself, it's incredibly important to be open-minded.

I believe the more open-minded someone is—the better, because it allows them to grow. The more open-minded someone is, the more likely they are to experience a new event or perspective. Accordingly, new experiences enable us to grow. Without new experiences we could not grow, because dogmatism would prevent it.

What causes dogmatism?

I would like to begin this chapter with a question: why do people become dogmatic? One of the main reasons is because dogmatism grounds someone in their idea of reality. On the contrary, by being open-minded, people are vulnerable to their idea of reality being changed or proven wrong.

As you may have noticed, a lot of people don't like change. Nor do people like to be proven wrong. Both experiencing change and being proven wrong can cause us to feel uncomfortable, as our idea and sense of being grounded within reality goes from order to chaos—or known to unknown. Hence, it's a lot easier for us to stick to what we already believe, because this grounds us in our own understanding of reality.

Dogmatism is often a word that comes up when people are discussing controversial topics such as religion or politics. The reason for this is because both religion and politics are common ways for people to ground themselves in their understanding of reality. Thus the reason why these can be very controversial topics to debate or discuss.

The effect of labels

When we ground ourselves, we often create an identity for ourselves. For example, if religion gives you a deep understanding of reality, then you may identify as a Catholic or a Muslim. If politics gives you a strong sense of grounding, then you may identify as a Republican or a Democrat. When you ground yourself, it's important to be mindful of the type of labels that you give yourself.

Labels help us to identify and categorize things, objects, and people. Therefore, you should be very careful about the labels you place on yourself. Once you give yourself a label, you place yourself into a category, which gives you an image you must live up to.

I have a small saying that applies here: "One word can change an entire story; one word can change an entire life". For example, if you give yourself the label of a "goth", that places you into the category of "gothic subculture". Now you identify as a goth and are part of goth culture, you must live up to a certain image to fit in. For example, wearing all black and listening to a certain genre of music such as gothic rock. To give yourself the label of a goth but not live

How to Think Inde pendently

up to the image of a goth can create social problems for you. Labelling yourself as a goth also means it will be difficult to relate to non-goths. And not living up to the image of a goth makes it difficult to relate to real goths. The lesson here is: don't promote a life that you don't live, as doing so can get you into a lot of trouble.

You now have a good understanding of why identity is so important to people. If you want to understand people's actions, you must understand that we want other people to see us as we see ourselves. For example, if someone identifies as a Catholic, then they want other people to see them as being faithful to God and Jesus Christ. When other people see us as we see ourselves, it reinforces the beliefs we have about ourselves, and this can include both positive and negative beliefs.

The effect of identity

Another thing to keep in mind is this: once someone has an identity that provides them with perceived success in life (such as money, fame, or power), it can be hard to let go of that identity. Once someone is rewarded for having a certain identity, it can be very difficult to give up.

For example, if someone comes from an abusive home and lives in poverty, they may give themselves the identify of a criminal or a gangster. They label themselves as a gangster and live the lifestyle of a criminal. This rewards them with acceptance from their peers (other gang members or criminals) and money. Accordingly, it can be hard to give up this identity and form a new identity. The criminal identity can be very rewarding, and people can feel comfortable with this identity. However, once someone is labelled and identified as a criminal it can be very difficult for them to live a normal life uninvolved with crime. Because not many employers want to hire an employee with a criminal background.

Our identity plays a big role in the choices we make in life. Because our identity is so important to us, it can cause people to become dogmatic towards anything that opposes or threatens their identity. To avoid this, it's important to be open-minded towards other people's perspectives. Doing so allows you to understand their identity and how they view the world. On the other hand, dogmatism leads us to become offended by other people's perspectives. When we are being dogmatic, perspectives that don't align with our own become threatening to us. And once a perspective becomes threatening, we feel the need to defend our own perspective against it.

For example, Catholics believe that Jesus Christ was the son of God, which is the Catholic perspective. However, if you were to present a Catholic with the perspective that Jesus was not the son of God and was merely a normal man, perhaps even a Buddhist, this perspective would cause the Catholic to become defensive about their beliefs. The perspective of Jesus not being the son of God goes against the Catholic's understanding and beliefs on how reality works.

Avoiding dogmatism

To avoid being dogmatic, you must open yourself to new ideas. If you close yourself to new ideas, you close yourself off from discovering better ways of living. Remaining dogmatic will also cause you to become easily offended or defensive about your beliefs.

To avoid being dogmatic, I encourage you to reflect inwardly on areas of your life where you get easily offended or defensive. Ask yourself: why do I get so defensive when someone challenges my perspective on this topic or area? To begin to extract dogmatism from your life, you must be completely honest with yourself. Dogmatism can be a shield that allows us to avoid being honest with ourselves. So instead of investigating a personal belief, we instead assume that what we believe is true without any evidence or facts. If you don't reflect inwardly, you reflect outwardly, meaning instead of finding fault internally, you will find fault externally.

When we are proven wrong, it leaves us with two choices. The first choice is to admit that our perception of reality was wrong. The second choice is to claim that the other person's perception of reality is wrong. In other words, you'll either admit that your perception of reality is wrong or you will find fault externally.

When pursuing open-mindedness, you must accept and be comfortable with the possibility that you could be wrong in what you believe. This is not an easy thing to do for a lot of people. Being proven wrong on something causes your perception of reality to shift, which can be a very uncomfortable experience to go through.

Have you ever been completely certain about something only to find out later that you were wrong? I have, and I would put good money on the fact that you have too. Do you remember how it felt? To have a concept or notion of how you thought reality works and it being completely shattered. It leaves us confused and shocked, with a strange discomfort that we can't seem to shake off, as we fall from order into chaos.

If you're a student of history, you may have noticed all the times that society and individuals were wrong. For example, people once believed the earth was flat, or that the sun rotated around the earth. People believed that you could die riding a train at high speed. Not to mention the countless times the world was predicted to end.

In fact, everything you believe is determined by the location and time you were born. For example, if you were born in Ancient Greece, you would be taught and led to believe that there were multiple gods and goddesses, such as Zeus, Athena, Hades, Apollo, and Ares. You would most likely pray and commit sacrifices in their name, as was normal at the time.

A more modern example is North Korea. Imagine you were born in North Korea. You would be told that Kim Jong-un was a god. You would believe that your country was under threat of invasion by U.S. troops. And depending on your social class, you may not even know that the internet exists. Your country, culture, and time of birth determine your worldview and what you believe is true.

Questions: Worldview

- If I had been born in another country, how would my perception of the world be different?
- Is it likely that some of the beliefs I hold could be wrong?
- In what ways am I dogmatic?
- How can I be more open-minded?
- How has being dogmatic caused me problems?
- In what ways do I ground myself in reality?
- What are some identities that I give myself?
- Do I promote a life I do not live?

Chapter Five
How to Stand up for Yourself

Not caring what other people think about you is a double-edged sword, but many of us don't realise that. The first side of the sword, which you may be familiar with, is not caring about the negative opinions of others. This goes along the lines of not allowing other people's negative opinions to affect your self-esteem, nor allowing such opinions to guide your life. However, the same can be said for the other side of the sword—you shouldn't allow the positive opinions of others to get to your head either.

Other people's opinions

Yes, positive opinions and feedback can be good for our self-esteem and encourage us to be braver, granting us courage. By no means am I saying that you should ignore all positive opinions or feedback. Just be aware that positive opinions and feedback can be as deadly as negative ones. This sounds strange, because at first glance positive opinions are an indicator that you're doing the correct thing, right? The answer is *not always*.

I find there to be a darker side to positive feedback and opinions. In fact, I invented my own word "conmomus" (pronounced *con-mom-us*) to describe what I mean. "Con" stands for condition, while "momus" comes from the Greek Momus, who was the god of mockery, satire, blame, and criticism. Some people say I can't go around inventing my own words, but I just did. The definition of "conmomus" is when a person blames or criticises someone for their actions to cause guilt—in order to manipulate or change their actions, and then praises any newly changed actions. In other words, conmomus is a form of peer pressure.

For illustration, consider a school student who enjoys playing video games in their spare time. It's the end of the day and they've finished all of their school work, so they decide to relax by playing a video game. However, their parent walks in and says "Why are you playing video games? You should be studying." This causes the student to feel guilty for playing games. The next day, the student has finished all of the required school work for that day, but instead of relaxing and playing video games, they continue studying. Now, when their parent walks in, they praise the student for studying and not playing games. Even though the student is unhappy and unable to relax, they continue to study and do something they don't want to do due to feeling guilty.

Standing up for yourself

The next time you find yourself in a similar situation, I recommend taking the opportunity to learn to stand up for yourself. A lot of people find it difficult to stand up for themselves, as it can be an anxiety-provoking experience. Note, standing up for yourself doesn't mean being rude or aggressive towards other people. Standing up for yourself means making it clear that you have boundaries and conditions. In chapter 6, I'll talk about how to set up boundaries and conditions for yourself.

The key to standing up for yourself is never allowing someone else to silence or control your personality. Your personality, even though it may be different and unique, is a beautiful thing. Just because someone else (such as a friend, co-worker, or family member) doesn't like your personality, this doesn't give them the right to tell you who you are and what you should be doing with your time.

It's sad to say, but the people you're closest to will often be the ones to tell you what you can and can't do, whether it's a parent, sibling, boyfriend, girlfriend, husband, or wife, and even our best friends. Sometimes, they push limiting beliefs on us, causing us to feel guilty about who we are and to think that something is wrong with the way we are. This leads to conmomus or crippled self-esteem.

Therefore, what you need to do is stand up for yourself and make it clear that you have boundaries and that your time is your own. You can do this by having time dedicated to others while also having a separate amount of time carved out of your day for you. The best tool to achieve this is communication.

Communication is key

For illustration, if your parents or teachers are overly strict, simply have a one-on-one conversation with them and tell them the situation you're in. If you don't communicate your problems, it's impossible for the other person to understand your situation or for the situation to improve.

When entering a conversation with someone, it's important to know what exactly you want to achieve. It's also important to go into the conversation understanding the other person's point of view, which is why it's so vital to be open-minded. Sometimes, you'll find that the reason someone is strict with you is because they care for you the most and being strict is their way of preparing you for life. The goal of the conversation should be to find a middle ground or a solution that everyone is happy with.

Discussing the issue may also enable both parties to correct any misunderstandings about the other. For example, perhaps the reason your parents tell you to stop playing videos games and go back to studying is because they're under the impression that you haven't finished all of your school work and are being lazy. If you communicate with them and help them understand that you've finished all of the required work, they may be less strict and allow you to play. Plus, they may not understand that you're stressed out and need time to relax and enjoy yourself. Communication is key when you're standing up for yourself, as without it nothing will change.

Developing confidence

Standing up for yourself requires confidence, and it can be difficult to build up the confidence to do this. This begs the question, how can I be more confident in myself? A big part of confidence comes from experience, which creates its own problem when you're young because you haven't had the chance to gain that experience yet.

What do I mean by experience? Remember the first day of high school and how nerve-racking that was? New school, new students, new teachers, and harder work. In your old school, you were one of the older students, but in high school you're now one of the youngest. The first day or even week of high school can be scary, because it's the unknown. You don't have much experience, and therefore it's normal to feel unconfident.

Fast forward a couple of months and high school no longer feels scary. You have complete confidence in attending school. This is because experience builds confidence. The more you do something, the better you get at it—and this includes standing up for yourself. The first time you stand up for yourself, it's scary and nerve-racking. Your heart starts racing and you feel your adrenaline kick in. But the more you do it and the more experience you have, this will give you natural confidence to stand up for yourself.

If you're having a difficult time building confidence, other than gaining more experience, I recommend working out and eating a healthy diet. Regular exercise and eating a nutritional diet can do wonders in building self-confidence. Working out will help you feel good about yourself, as it improves your self-image. Eating a nutritional diet helps you feel good by giving you more energy. Together, they naturally increase your confidence—with the added benefit of improved health.

Exercise: Standing up for yourself

Write down the areas of your life where you believe you need to stand up for yourself. It may be one or two areas, or even ten. Write down as many as you feel are necessary. Once you've identified these areas, start a one-on-one conversation with the person you feel is not respecting your personality. While it may feel intimating at first, when you get more experience over time, it won't feel as intimating. Instead, it will be a natural response to stand up for yourself.

Keep in mind that other people are intitled to their own opinions. However, that doesn't give them the right to be disrespectful towards you. Nor does it give you the right to be disrespectful towards them.

Questions: Standing up for yourself
- In what ways can I stand up for myself?
- Will I commit to being more confident in life?
- In what ways do other people silence and control my personality?
- Am I living the life I want or the life that somebody else wants for me?
- Who is it that I want to be?

When you're young, it's difficult to figure out who you *want* to be, and not who you think you should be. Who you want to be and who you should be will overlap with one another. Part of you will want to be independent and do your own thing in life. The other part will feel under pressure to do what society and your parents expect you to do. Therefore, it's important to stand up for yourself—otherwise you risk other people dictating your life. If that happens, then you end up living someone else's life instead of your own.

Chapter Six
Toxic and Negative People

In this chapter, we'll look at your relationships with negative and toxic people. Your relationships will be the true test of how well you're able to think independently and remain independent. Thinking independently does not mean being a lone wolf isolated from society. Rather, thinking independently is about remaining in society without it controlling or conditioning you. Your relationships will have a large influence on how you think and how you behave. This is where thinking independently comes into play, as it enables you to control your surroundings and environment.

Toxic people

If you allow toxic people into your life, they will poison your mind, and in return, your mind will poison your life. Personally, I've had a lot of experience dealing with negative and toxic people, as like many others I've worked in customer service. Working with the general public on a day-to-day basis takes a strong mentality, and I take my hat off to those who work in such jobs every day.

Before I began working for myself, I used to work at the landfill, where I would interact with hundreds of customers a day. This meant it wasn't uncommon for me to come face to face with toxic and abusive customers. In fact, customers like this were so common at the landfill that staff were required to undergo yearly training to deal with difficult and toxic customers. Toxic people can ruin your life and influence your mind and thinking in a negative way. Therefore, an important part of independent thinking is recognising when you're in a toxic relationship. Thanks to my years of training and experience, here are five steps to deal with toxic people in your life.

Step 1: Identify the toxic, negative person

The first step is to identify the toxic, negative person in your life. This could be any of the following:

- Your boss
- Co-workers
- Business partners
- Clients
- Customers
- Wife/husband
- Girlfriend/boyfriend
- Family members
- YouTube content creator
- Music artist
- Celebrities
- And most commonly, your friends

Just because you haven't met someone in real life doesn't mean they can't impact you in a negative way. Therefore, it's important to be mindful of the type of content you consume while on the internet. Once you've identified the toxic person, begin to observe their behaviour and how they make you feel. Do they make you feel good and positive about yourself? Or do they make you feel anxious, sad, or angry?

Common traits associated with toxic and negative people include:
- Playing the victim
- Depression
- Anger
- Violence
- Being dramatic
- Pessimism
- Close-mindedness (thinking that nothing is going to change)
- Criminality
- Low self-development (doesn't believe in self-improvement)
- Having an addiction (such as alcohol or drugs)
- Placing their interests in front of yours
- Trying to manipulate you
- Pushing fear onto you
- Encouraging you to judge others
- Constantly making you feel guilty or ashamed of yourself

These are a few of the common traits associated with toxic and negative people that you should be aware of. If you observe someone within your life with these traits, then it's time to move on to step two.

Step 2: Avoid the blame game

At the time of writing this, the world's population is 7.6 billion people. That's 7.6 billion different perspectives. With so many different perspectives, it's very easy for problems to arise due to conflicting points of view. It becomes all too easy for us to reflect outwardly when something goes wrong, which it always does. And when something does go wrong and a problem occurs, we play the blame game.

What is the blame game you ask? The game plays along the lines of "I am not the problem, they are." Or "If it wasn't for them, I wouldn't be having such problems." Followed by thoughts of "If only they would change, things would be so much better", or "How do they not realise that what they believe is wrong and what I believe is correct?"

Nothing gets people's blood boiling more than the blame game. With so many serious problems in the world, you'd think that playing games would be a waste of time. However, turn on the news, scroll down your social media feed, or watch a controversial YouTube video and visit the comment section—and you will see the blame game live in action.

The blame game will hinder your health and waste your time, so I advise you not to play it. Instead, understand that everything is perspective and blaming another person is simply a waste of time. Playing the blame game doesn't get you anywhere, which is a good reason not to play it.

Yes, it's easier to blame other people than it is to take responsibility. However, I suggest you try to avoid doing that, because that's how a lot people get stuck in life. They get so caught up in blaming people who have done them wrong that they never move on with their own life. Instead of blaming another for the problems in your life, I encourage you to reflect inwardly instead of outwardly and take the responsibility upon yourself to fix the problem within. Don't blame the other person—rather forgive and understand.

This is the reason why I believe the Bible teaches forgiveness, because holding a grudge and hating the person who has done you wrong only hurts you. I believe that forgiving others benefits you more than the other person.

You see, it's very easy to sabotage your own life by holding on to blame and not accepting responsibility. But in blaming the other person, you're giving up your power. You're waiting for them to change and make a difference. In other words, if they don't change, you won't change.

Blaming someone else is another form of playing the victim role —by giving your power away to other people, you become the victim. It's a vicious circle. With no power to change, people often blame others for their situation. They start to tell themselves and others that their lives would be better if they had this or that, or if it wasn't for that one person, they would be happier. These are the cries of the victim, helpless and lost.

By refusing to play the victim, taking back your own power, and deciding to change yourself, you can improve the situation.

Step 3: Create boundaries

Once you've identified a toxic person and are willing to take responsibility for the situation, then it's time to create boundaries between you and them. To create a boundary, make it clear to them that you have standards and boundaries. By doing this, you're setting up conditions and requirements for how you expect to be treated and respected.

To make it clear, the next time that person is negative towards you, warn them that you won't tolerate or allow such negative and toxic behaviour. This will make them aware that you've had enough. If you don't set boundaries for yourself, then you're allowing the toxic person to walk all over you.

A small word of advice: don't allow the toxic person to make you feel guilty for trying to stand up for yourself. Guilt tactics are a common method used by toxic people to keep control over their victims. When a toxic person feels that they're losing control over their victim, they often implement guilt tactics or even turn to threats.

Step 4: Cut them out of your life

In most cases, creating boundaries between you and the toxic person is good for solving small disputes. However, sometimes creating boundaries is not enough. If the person you're dealing with continues to disrespect your boundaries and conditions, then it may be time to cut them out of your life.

To cut the toxic person out, cease all contact and communication with them. This might include removing them as a friend on social media, unsubscribing, changing jobs, moving location, etc. Of course, changing jobs and moving location is easier said than done. However, if it's something you feel *needs* to be done, then it should be a project to work on over time.

Step 5: If you can't cut them out of your life

I understand that you may be saying "But what if I can't cut the toxic person out of my life?" If you can't cut the toxic person out of your life, it indicates that you're still dependent or reliant on them in some way or another, such as your parents, or that you're relying on something you're both involved in, for example, the same place of work or a sports team.

If this is the case, I advise you to start planning and finding a way to be less dependent on the toxic person or the environment you're both in. If it's a family member, limiting the amount of contact you have with them by creating boundaries is a good first step. Reduce the amount of time you spend interacting and engaging with them. Instead, spend that time self-improving or with supportive friends and family who respect your boundaries.

Sometimes, toxic people just need help, and giving them the required help, such as rehab, or helping them improve their own life can go a long way. But remember, keep your boundaries while you help them—otherwise they could drag you down with them.

Questions: *Dealing with negative people*

- Who are the negative and toxic people in my life?
- Are these people aware that they are being negative and toxic towards other people?
- In what ways can I be negative and toxic towards other people?
- In what ways can I improve myself to be less negative and toxic?
- Am I negative and toxic towards myself?

- If yes, why am I so negative and toxic towards myself (e.g. are you blaming yourself for something you did?)
- Will you forgive yourself?

Now you know how to deal with negative and toxic people through a step-by-step guide, so start doing it. Knowing how to deal with toxic people is a key ingredient to thinking independently, so even though it might feel difficult to cut negative people out of your life, it's better for you in the long run.

Chapter Seven
Relationships and Self-love

Relationships and self-love play a large part in you thinking independently. Self-love is vital, because if you don't love yourself, you won't look after yourself, then you risk sabotaging your ability to think independently.

What's more, if you don't love and respect yourself, then you're left relying on someone else for that love and respect, and you will always be a slave to that love and respect. You must accept and love yourself before you can share acceptance and love with others. It's good to receive love and respect from others, but not to the point where it controls and limits your life. Your personal relationships with others largely influence how you think and act. This is why it's important to understand your relationships with others.

Intentions in relationships

There are two reasons why people get into relationships. The first reason is because the other person has something they want. In relationships, both parties want to exact something from the other, such as sex, money, status, not feeling alone, etc. The second reason is to share something with the other person, such as sex, love, life experiences, family, etc.

When entering a relationship, you must ask yourself: what is the reason behind me entering this relationship? Am

I trying to exact something from the other person or am I trying to share something with them? This includes all types of relationships: friendships, romantic, business, etc.

If you decide to enter a relationship with the intent to extract, you've automatically placed an expiry date on that relationship. Because like a small pond, there is only so much water you can drain before it runs dry. It could take a day, a week, a month, a year, or even 10 years—but eventually the pond will run dry. So, I encourage you to create relationships that are based on sharing and not exacting. Sharing the experience of travelling around the world with someone you love is much more fulfilling than sharing it with someone who is just with you for your wealth.

Once you know your own intentions, the next step is finding someone with the same intentions as you. If one person in the relationship is trying to extract while the other is trying to share, an imbalance is created. In this case, the well will run dry. Thus, it's important to ensure that both members in a relationship have the same intent towards each other. Otherwise, the relationship will have an expiry date. The only way a relationship can last in the long term is if both members are trying to share. A good question to ask is: how do I share without extracting from the other person? And the answer to this question is self-love.

Self-love

What is self-love, you ask? Self-love is not selfishness; rather, it's treating yourself with respect and empathy, while being patient and understanding with yourself. To not extract from the other person, you must acknowledge that you are a complete person by yourself. *You* are responsible for all your happiness.

You must accept yourself for who you are—and only once you've accepted yourself can you accept another without trying to change them. If you're trying to change someone else, then you don't love them the way they are. You either love them for who they are—or you don't.

So, you must accept yourself before you can accept another. If you have trouble accepting yourself, this is a sign that you must start practicing self-love. Practicing self-love can be difficult, because a lot of people don't like themselves. When people don't like themselves, they neglect their own happiness. And once they start to neglect their own happiness, it doesn't take long for them to spiral downwards. Hence the importance of self-love.

To practice self-love, you must change any anger or hatred you have for yourself and turn it into love. The next time you make a mistake, don't become upset with yourself or call yourself names. Instead, accept that it was a mistake and love yourself. For example, if you fail at an important exam, don't put yourself down or criticise yourself. Just accept that you made a mistake and need to improve.

However, improving does *not* mean punishing yourself by overworking or setting unachievable standards. Improving means identifying the areas that need fixing, then working on them over time, without punishing yourself. If you feel the need to punish yourself—don't. Instead, feel love towards the part of yourself that is trying to punish and resist you. Love is something that you must practice, and it is only by practicing love that you can ever feel loved. Self-love is about accepting everything about yourself and not resisting yourself.

Self-love the way you look

An area of self-love that many people struggle with in modern times is the way their body looks. Instead of loving who they are and what their body looks like, they judge and criticise their appearance and constantly try to change their body. Do not judge or criticise your body. Your body is perfect the way it is, and cannot be any other way than the way it is now.

However, self-love also means looking after your own body. So don't neglect it by living an unhealthy lifestyle. Instead, show your body love and look after it by eating healthy and exercising. If you're not doing that right now, then don't berate yourself for it. Just accept it, see where you need to improve your lifestyle to be healthier, and love yourself.

Understand this: the problem is not with your body—the problem is with your mind. Your mind is projecting all of these conditions and judgements on how your body should appear. The mind often gets these ideas from social media, television, friends, and culture to name just a few. What you must realise is that these projections from the mind onto the body are only thoughts. And because these projections are just thoughts, you can change these thoughts or pay no attention to them. If you don't give your negative thoughts attention, they will naturally go away.

Self-sabotage

Self-love is a powerful tool to prevent you from sabotaging yourself. The reason we sabotage ourselves is because we are trying to resist some part of ourselves, but this causes us even more harm. The way we sabotage us is by judging ourselves. We continually judge and criticise our thoughts and actions, as they continually fail to meet our expectations.

The reason why we may resist a part of ourselves is because we are comparing that part to something else that we consider "better" or "perfect". For illustration, I once had a conversation with a young woman who was aspiring to be a model. As we were discussing her modelling career, she said she didn't like the look of her nose. She insisted it was ugly and too large and wanted surgery to correct its appearance. I replied that her nose was perfectly normal and surgery was unnecessary. Then I asked her why she felt this way. She got her phone out and showed me pictures of other models, pointing out that their noses were smaller and beautiful. She was comparing the way her nose looked to someone else's nose. Consequently, she began to resist and reject that part of herself.

Resisting a part of ourselves doesn't just relate to physical appearances—it can also be emotional. For example, we don't feel that we're a good enough person to be loved or accepted. This is why someone may feel insecure about who they are as a person and hide their true personality. Accordingly, self-love involves accepting who you are and not judging yourself.

So how do you stop self-judgement? First, you must start by not judging others. When you judge another person, you're also judging yourself. For example, if you judge someone for being fat, you're also judging yourself, because you subconsciously create rules for yourself. If you gain a bit of weight, you begin to compare yourself to that person and the judgements you made about them. In other words, once you've judged or criticised an image, your mind will do everything it can to prevent your self-image from relating to the criticised, disowned image. The closer the two images get, the more you suffer.

Exercise: Judgements

1. Write down all of the judgements you have about yourself.
2. Then write down all of the judgements you have about other people.
3. Try to make both lists as long as you possibly can.
4. Go through both lists of judgements and you will find matching judgements. For example, a judgement of someone else may be "The sound of her voice is annoying", whereas a self-judgement might be "I don't like the sound of my own voice".
5. See how many matches you can make.
6. Once you've found all of the matches, identify the five biggest judgments on both lists. These will be subjective. In other words, they are the judgements *you feel* are the worst.
7. You can now begin to work on preventing yourself from using those judgements.
8. Once you've gone through the first five, move on to the next five until you have no more judgements left.

Questions: Judgements

- In what ways can I be toxic and negative?
- In my relationships, am I trying to extract from the other person or share with them?
- In what ways do I judge other people?
- In what ways do I judge myself?
- Why do I judge so much?

- What does love mean to me?
- Do I love myself?
- If I don't love myself, why do I continue to resist myself?
- What is stopping me from loving and accepting myself unconditionally?
- Why am I resisting parts of myself?

Chapter Eight
How to Find Your Life Purpose

To not follow a path is to become lost, and to follow the wrong path is to arrive at an undesired destination. I would like to begin this chapter discussing the meaning and reason to life. Understanding the meaning and reason for life will help you find your life purpose. In life, you will hear (and probably have heard) multiple answers to the meaning and purpose to life. The problem is: this is someone else's meaning and purpose in life—and not necessarily yours. To think independently is to find and develop your own meaning and purpose in life, which is something you decide and no one else. By the end of this chapter, you will know how to find your own meaning and purpose in life.

The reason for life

Firstly, don't confuse the reason for life with the *meaning* of life. The reason for life is that we, as humans, evolved. If we didn't evolve, we wouldn't live in the world that we live in now, and you wouldn't be reading this book. In our case, evolution is a quality answer to the reason for life and why we are here. Of course, if you're religious, then the reason for life from your perspective would be God or a god.

Therefore, what is the meaning of life? The meaning of life is **belief**. In other words, the meaning of life is whatever you believe it to be. If you believe the meaning of life is to serve God, then that is your meaning of life. If your meaning of life is to sing and dance, then that is your meaning of life.

To have a fulfilling purpose in life, your life purpose must be parallel with your meaning of life. If your meaning of life and life purpose are not parallel, then you will be left empty and unfulfilled. Just think of all the people you know who are unfulfilled. This is because their life purpose and life meaning are not parallel. For example, if serving your country gives you meaning in life, then working a regular 9 to 5 job won't bring you fulfilment, even if it pays well. If serving your country is your meaning of life, then working in the military or politics will bring you greater fulfilment than a regular job. So, you must find a life purpose that allows you to pursue your meaning of life. If you don't currently know what your meaning of life is, I advise you to find it.

Finding your meaning of life

To find your meaning of life, simply reflect inwardly and question yourself. Question your beliefs, life values, ideologies, and perspectives. There is no meaning to your life magically floating around in the universe. Rather, the meaning of your life is something that comes from *within* you. It is something you must create for yourself.

Your meaning of life should not be rational—rather, it should be completely emotional, something that feels right to you. Your meaning of life must be something that you feel to be true. You can only find a true meaning of life by searching your emotions. A completely rational approach to finding meaning in life will lead you to nihilism*. If you choose to hold a nihilistic perspective towards your life, you will be left unfulfilled, as denying that you have meaning in life leads to a purposeless life. We'll look at this in more depth later in the chapter.

Your meaning in life must make you emotional, because it is emotion that builds passion and it is emotion that allows you to be fulfilled in life. However, keep in mind that money is not a meaning of life, nor are any materialistic goods. Materialism is only good at making a life look good from the outside.

Once you have discovered and found meaning within your life, then you can begin to work on your life purpose. You use your emotions to find your meaning within life, then you use your rationality to construct a purpose within your life. In the next chapter, we'll look in-depth at how to create an impactful life purpose. For now, you need to understand what it is.

Understanding life purpose

Your life purpose is something you must create. It's your choice alone and no one else can decide for you. Your life purpose is something that you choose—it's not something that is given to you. If your life purpose is handed to you, then it's merely someone else's life purpose pushed onto you. Religion is a good example of this. A preacher or priest tells people their life purpose, which is to serve Jesus Christ as lord and saviour. While I appreciate that religion can give people purpose in life, corrupt individuals can easily manipulate that purpose. Hence the reason I am so passionate about teaching people how to choose and find their own meaning and purpose in life—one that comes from *within*. When your meaning and purpose in life is something you have decided yourself, it's much more difficult for other people to manipulate that.

The life purpose you choose can be anything you want it to be; however, it must be parallel with your meaning of life. It's extremely important that your meaning of life and your life purpose align with each other. Specifically, your life purpose should aim at your meaning of life. For example, if being a parent to your children would give you meaning in life, then your life purpose should aim at that meaning. So, your life purpose might be to ensure that your children receive the best possible future, such as getting them into the best schools and universities or moving to another country to give them opportunities you never had.

To have a fulfilling life purpose, it must be a purpose that aims at your meaning of life. Your meaning of life is the destination, while your life purpose is the vehicle that helps you arrive at that destination. Your meaning of life is built from emotion, while your life purpose is built from rationality. Together, they make the perfect equilibrium.

Multiple meanings

When you're deciding these things, a question that may arise is "Can I have multiple meanings or purposes in my life?" This is a very good question. We often have an image in our mind that we only get one big meaning of life and one big life purpose. It's often portrayed this way in movies and books. For example, the meaning of life is enlightenment, therefore my only life purpose is to meditate.

However, what I have discovered is that it's okay to have more than one meaning and purpose in life. You can have more than one meaning of life and more than one life purpose. In fact, you can have as many as you want. For illustration, if defending the law and being a good parent to your children gives you meaning in life, then your first life purpose could be becoming the best lawyer in the country, and your other life purpose could be being a good parent. The trick to having multiple life purposes is being able to *balance* them. You can have as many life purposes as you want, but you must keep in mind that you only have so much time within a day.

Difficult questions

Remember that your meaning of life can only be found within you, so to find it, you must search within your feelings. However, when seeking your meaning of life and creating a life purpose, you might encounter some difficult emotions that try to lead you astray. For example, what if you want to create a life purpose to cause the most amount of chaos and harm possible? Or what if you don't believe in anything and think that life is meaningless?

Firstly, creating a destructive life purpose is a bad idea. Just imagine how horrible society would be if everyone's life purpose was to cause harm and chaos to others. It wouldn't be a very nice place to live or a place you'd want your family and friends to live in, would it?

Secondly, nihilism is not a practical philosophy to use when creating a life purpose. A nihilist would say "Well, life is meaningless, so it doesn't really matter what happens to other people or to the world." This gives the nihilist a good excuse to not create a life purpose, and means they remain free from all responsibility. Especially when they believe they're just another number in the human population.

However, such a notion is fundamentally flawed, because we're all part of a network. As a human being, you're a person in a network and what you do affects the other people connected to you. Social media is a perfect example of this.

Accordingly, what you do *does* matter, because it affects other people—whether you realise it or not. Your actions and words have both positive and negative consequences towards the other people you're connected to, which also affects the people they're connected too.

Just because life is meaningless for the nihilist doesn't mean it's meaningless for other people. Your actions *will* affect other people in ways that you can't comprehend. This means that the things you do and don't do matter a lot more than you think. Once you become aware of this, you'll realise that everything you do matters. And this also means you have to accept the responsibility associated with that.

Especially when you're young, nihilism is a poor philosophy to adopt and follow, because you're deciding the direction your life will head in. Small changes now make big differences in the future. This means you must be careful in how you treat others and what you do daily.

If you create a destructive life purpose or try to avoid having a life purpose, you cause misery to yourself and others around you. This is a trap that a lot of people easily fall into. They avoid all responsibility because they believe this will lead them to comfort. However, when they avoid all responsibility, everything becomes meaningless and they end up miserable. I promise you there is no comfort in misery.

To find your meaning of life, you must look inside yourself and connect with your emotions, but realise that you may have more than one meaning. Your life purpose must run in parallel to your meaning of life. This leads to the question: how do I create a meaningful and impactful life purpose? We'll look at how to do that in the next chapter.

Chapter Nine
Creating an Impactful Life Purpose

As you saw in the last chapter, your meaning of life should be completely emotional, whereas your life purpose should be completely rational. To create a successful life purpose, you need to think deeply and logically about the future. This way, you build a life purpose that you truly want, not what somebody else has pushed onto you. This is the importance of thinking independently.

Look within

Your life purpose can be anything you want it to be; however, there is a catch. Only *you* can design and create your life purpose. People like me can only guide you in the right direction and give you advice. The ins and outs of your life purpose is your task alone. There is no magical YouTube video, book, or guru out there that will tell you step by step how to find your life purpose. The best they can do is give you guidance and advice. Instead, you must look deep within, so start by asking yourself questions.

Questions: Life purpose

- What do I want?
- What do I want to achieve in life?
- What are my strengths and weakness?

- What is required of me?
- Do I have what it takes to commit to my own goals?

Is money a purpose?

A big mistake that many people make, especially young people, is choosing a life purpose that is solely about making money. So the only reason they want to run a business is to drive an expensive car, wear designer clothes, live in a big mansion, and date hot women or men.

Don't get me wrong—I'm not saying that running a business for those reasons is *necessarily* a bad thing. However, I am saying that such a life purpose will not make you fulfilled. And why not, you may ask? Because such a life purpose will have you continually chasing materialistic items. It normally starts small, such as buying a pair of expensive shoes, but next time it's an expensive watch, then a car, then a house, then a jet, then another house. At the end, you're left working long hours, only to continue consuming. This is why people who live such a life are often left with a form of unfulfillment that they can't get rid of.

Of course, I'm not against people having nice things and lots of money. But what I'm saying is: if you make money or material objects your life purpose, then you're going to be left unfulfilled. All of that being said, you may still make money your life purpose, and that will be the only way for you to understand that it doesn't lead to fulfilment.

Is purpose an end goal?

Another common mistake is believing that a fulfilling life purpose is about the reward or the end goal. For example, money, material items, accolades, and titles are the result of hard work, meaning they're the reward you get for working hard. However, a life purpose that is about rewards and end goals will leave you unfulfilled, because there will always be another desirable reward or material object for you to chase.

On the contrary, a fulfilling life purpose is about *the process*. If you want a fulfilling life purpose, then you have to love and enjoy the process. It should be the process that gets you out of bed in the morning, not the reward.

The reason I write books is not to publish them and make money. Rather, it's because I love teaching and writing. I enjoy thinking and writing for 10 to 14 hours a day, and it's what I love to do. This is where a lot of wannabe authors fail. They say they want to write a book, yet they're more interested in the reward that comes from selling the book than they are about writing it.

The same can be said of business. Many people go into business with the reward in mind, such as the flash car or to call themselves a CEO. This creates a problem, because once it's time to start the process of running the business, they're not interested, and they remain a dreamer.

If you want to create a successful life purpose, it's extremely important that you love the process of what you're doing. That you love it in and of itself, not for the reward or end goal. Otherwise, you're going to be left miserable.

Of course, it's great to receive rewards for your hard work, and if you want to buy a Rolls Royce after 10 years of hard work, then go ahead. However, don't fall into the trap of creating a life purpose that revolves around reward. Instead, create a life purpose that revolves around the process—with rewards being the cherry and sprinkles on top.

How big should my purpose be?

Another question that may arise when deciding on your life purpose (or purposes) is: how big should I go? The answer is: don't be afraid to create large life purposes for yourself. If becoming the next president or prime minister of your country is meaningful to you, then set the goal and pursue it. Because you're only limited by the standards and goals that you set yourself.

As you've seen, I want to encourage you to do what you want to do in life and not what other people want you to do. If you want to live your own life, you have to create it yourself. However, I must warn you, there are hazards along the way when creating your own path in life. And a major one of these hazards is **fear**.

The reason why many people live an unsatisfied life is because they're stuck by fear. They're afraid that if they venture down the path of the unknown, which is who they really want to be, that they will fail. So, what do these people do instead? They settle for what's safe. They settle for what they should be instead of who they want to be. They stay in their comfort zone, on the safe path.

Well, let me share a secret with you. Failure is a part of life, and it always leaves you with two paths to choose from. Both paths have failure en route, however only one path leads to the life you truly want. On the first path, you set goals for yourself that you will either fail or succeed at. However, no matter what happens, there is always the opportunity for you to succeed. On the second path, you don't set any goals, and therefore don't set any conditions for failure.

The problem with option two is that you will fail all the time, but you won't realise it. So, with option two, there is no possibility of success. This is really important to realise, because a lot of people don't like to know when they fail. Failure is painful, so instead of accepting when they fail, they keep themselves wilfully blind to it.

I've worked with many people in my life who picked option two, and they are some of the most miserable people I've ever met. They've spent their entire life running and hiding from failure and pain. Through drugs, alcohol, or distractions, such as casual relationships or an escape into technology. They go from job to job, in the desperate hope that this new job will somehow give them fulfilment and joy, but after a couple of months, they're looking for their next place of employment, and so the cycle continues.

Nobody can stop you from remaining wilfully blind, but if you choose to be in denial, you're not really avoiding failure. The reality is that you will be failing all the time, but you just won't know it. This can be a dangerous thing if you do it for too long, because eventually you will hit a point of no return—and that's a scary place to be in life.

You see, by running from pain and failure, you will incur even more pain and failure. To avoid suffering unnecessary pain and failure, you must face it head on. Think of pain and failure as some of those counterintuitive aspects of life. If you try to avoid it, you will incur more of it. If you face it head on, you will experience less of it.

Only by picking option one will you have the opportunity for fulfilment and bliss. So, it's best to pick option one, as that is the only path to being successful in achieving your life purpose. Don't limit the life you could have based on fear and limitations, and don't be afraid about creating conditions of failure for yourself.

How do I balance life with my life purpose?

It's important to understand that life is what you make of it and it's important not to waste your time. It's okay to have fun and relax, but now is the time to invest in your future. This brings up the question: how do you balance fun and leisure with work and responsibility? One solution is to have a schedule.

While it's tempting to think that a schedule is a punishment you place on yourself, it's better to see it as a tool to help you get the day that you want. By setting a schedule, it prevents you from aimlessly jumping from one activity to the next. A schedule gives your day order and creates a set of responsibilities that you need to fulfil to achieve your purpose.

You can create your schedule online using a free tool called Google Calendar. When creating your schedule, a good question to ask yourself is: how much time do I waste in a day? Followed by: how productive would my day be if I stopped wasting time? It's not uncommon for people to waste their time on social media, watching movies, or playing video games. When you become aware of just how much time you waste in a day, you have more control over the situation, meaning you can get the day that you want.

When reflecting to yourself on what you do daily, you'll begin to discover what is and isn't a priority for you. To discover what is a priority for you, simply look at your daily habits. The things you spend the most time on in a day are priorities for you. This is important to realise, because some people say that their work is their main priority, yet they spend more time on social media than working. This means that social media is their main priority, not working, as that's what they're spending most of their time doing. Words can lie, but actions cannot.

Lifestyle fit for purpose

Creating an impactful life purpose requires a certain lifestyle. If you don't currently have the right habits in place to fulfil your life purpose, then you must change your habits—otherwise your life will remain the same. A lifestyle is merely a collection of habits.

If your current lifestyle doesn't match your desired life purpose, you should start by changing your habits. Start by changing the small habits, such as leaving dirty dishes in the sink or not folding the washing. Then work your way up to the larger habits, such as the type of food you eat. For example, if you don't eat breakfast in the morning, then a good place to start is preparing overnight oats before you go to bed at night, so they're ready in the morning to eat cold or quickly heat up.

You see, anything is possible given the right mindset. Once you start getting a handle on the small to medium habits in your life, you'll start to notice large changes in your lifestyle. Changing your lifestyle sounds like a big thing, but it's not when you start small and work your way up. Once you begin creating your desired lifestyle, that enables you to chase your life purpose.

Questions: Be strategic

When developing your life purpose, it's important to be as strategic as possible. The more strategic you are, the better the chances of you creating a successful life purpose. Ask yourself the following:

- Have I gathered enough intelligence and information to start pursuing my life purpose?
- Do I have the correct resources?
- Do I have enough resources?
- Does my lifestyle support my purpose?
- Do I have the disciple to stay focused?
- What's the worst-case scenario?
- Am I prepared for the worst-case scenario?
- Does my life purpose parallel with my meaning to life?
- What is the difference between my dream and reality?
- In what ways will I try to sabotage myself?

Avoiding self-sabotage

The last question is the most important. The primary reason why people don't live the life they want is because they sabotage themselves. They do this by not taking responsibility for themselves, and either remaining wilfully blind or playing the victim role.

When you're creating your life purpose, the biggest obstacle you will encounter is yourself. You can only go as far as you're willing to take yourself. Therefore, it's critically important that you identify the ways you will try to sabotage yourself. Write down a list of the ways you will attempt to sabotage yourself. Then begin to create small plans or ways to avoid this self-sabotage.

For example, when you fail at a project, how will you avoid criticising yourself or becoming depressed? It may be by calling a friend, staying away from the alcohol cabinet, or not listening to sad, depressing music. Whatever the answer is for you, find a way to prevent you from sabotaging yourself.

In summary, your life purpose needs to be completely rational and to aim at your meaning of life. You must have the right lifestyle in place that enables you to enjoy the process of your life purpose. And you must remain mindful of the ways you will attempt to sabotage yourself and find ways to counteract these.

Chapter Ten
Down to Business

Statistics show that heart attacks happen the most between 4 a.m. and 10 a.m. on Monday mornings. One of the many contributors to heart attacks being stress (Postgraduate Medical Journal, 1986). It doesn't take much to connect the dots to see what's really happening here. People are working in jobs that are making them sick and stressed. In this chapter, we'll get down to business, so you can start thinking independently about the world of work and jobs.

Unfulfilling jobs

In modern society, billions of people work in jobs that they're not satisfied with, and that don't give them any type of fulfilment. They work in jobs that have no meaning, require long and boring hours, or cause more stress than bliss.

I used to do a job like this when I was in my early twenties, after the landfill. My job was to sell mattresses, answer phone calls, and build bed bases. At the time, I thought it was a step in the right direction, as I was leaving blue collar work for white collar work, even though my new sales job paid less.

I didn't have a car, nor could I drive, so I had to walk to and from work in 40-degree heat, which took about 40 minutes for each trip. By the time I got to work, I was hot and tired, and it didn't help knowing that ahead of me I had a full day of stacking shelves and building bed bases. The people I worked with were very friendly and always helped me when I needed it, but I quickly realised that I hated my job. I was extremely depressed and stressed, and the work I was doing made me miserable. It only took three months before I reached breaking point and quit.

When I left, I remember feeling a great weight lifted off my shoulders, and at that point, I decided that I would never work a 9 to 5 job ever again. I would rather be homeless and living on the streets than working another job that made me feel the way my sales job did. People will often tell you that getting a job is the only option or it's what you should do. But it's not the only option, and you should think about what you want to do in life and the way that you want to work.

Personally, I can't stand to work for other people, and it drives me crazy. Of course, I have no problem working with others in a team environment; I just hate being told how to do my job and how I should spend my time. This is why I've done everything in my power to work for myself—to gain my freedom.

If you find yourself in a similar position in life, where you wish to work for yourself but don't know how, then this chapter may be valuable to you. I have developed seven simple rules to point you in the right direction to working independently. Most of the rules tie in nicely with what you've learnt in the book so far.

Rule #1: Love the process

The first rule is clichéd but true—you have to do something that you love. In the previous chapter, we discussed why it's important to enjoy the process and not just aim for the reward, as that leads to fulfilment. It's also the case that if you don't love what you do, you're never going to do the work to the best of your ability, nor are you going to stand out in your profession.

For me, writing is something that I love. The reason I write isn't to publish books, but because it brings me bliss and peace of mind knowing that it helps people achieve their goals and improve their lives. My work really brings me fulfilment and satisfaction that no job in my past ever has. What's more, I truly am grateful to all of the people who buy my books, as they help me to live the life that I do, so I put my greatest efforts into helping them.

However, doing what you love doesn't necessarily mean you have to work for yourself. If you want to work for someone else doing a job that you love, and that makes you happy, then that is great. Alternatively, if you're like me in that you can't stand to work for a boss, then working for yourself is a big step in the right direction. It's about what works for you.

To find your dream job or start your dream business, it must fit into your meaning of life. For example, if your meaning of life is to save the environment and you love drawing, then the perfect job for you may be creating art that raises awareness of environmental issues. Whatever your dream job is, don't be afraid to get creative.

Rule #2: Know what you want

The second rule is knowing exactly what you want and how you're going to achieve it. It's one thing to love movies and acting, however it's an entirely different thing to have a plan and know exactly how to get on the big screen.

Your step-by-step game plan is something you have to figure out and create for yourself. While books can guide you in the right direction, it is *you* who must put the time and effort into executing your plan. No one else will do it for you, nor can they even if they wanted to.

By now, you have a good idea of how to find meaning and purpose in your life. Once you've decided on a meaning and purpose (or multiple meanings and purposes), you need to start setting goals. The best way to do this is by setting up a personal calendar and making it clear what you need to achieve today, as you saw with habits in the previous chapter.

The difference between a dreamer and a person who achieves their dream is that one acts and the other continues dreaming. When I worked at the landfill, I had a co-worker who was always talking about how they would start their own little business, and how it would be so much more relaxing and easier than working at the landfill. Two years later, they left the landfill to work at another regular job. I still see them from time to time, and they still tell me how they plan to start their business.

The lesson is: don't remain a dreamer—make your dreams come true. Because you can dream all you like, but eventually you're going to reach a point where you have to take a leap of faith and start acting on that dream. Another word of advice here: when setting your goals, it's a good idea not to tell too many people about them. Instead of telling people about them, start working on them. *Less talk and more action.*

When you're young, it's the best time to take big risks. When you're older, you have more responsibilities, such as a family to look after and a house. So, when you're young and free to take big risks, start a business or a large work project. Even if you fail, you gain valuable life experience—and this will always be more valuable than someone else's hearsay knowledge.

Rule #3: Think Differently

You've probably heard of the saying "think outside of the box", meaning to think differently, unconventionally, or from a new perspective. An important part of business is thinking differently and being one step ahead of your competitors. In business, if you copy your competitors, you will always be one step behind, and your business will never be unique.

To be truly unique in business and find your own niche within a marketplace, you must be willing to think, and act differently compared to everyone else. Thinking and acting differently can be a frightening experience, because you're moving away from what's safe and known into the unknown. Moving into the unknown in business often means big risk; however, with big risk comes big reward.

Accordingly, to stand out among the competition, you must be willing to take on risks to try new things. If you never take any risks, your business will be mediocre and not unique. So, don't be afraid to try new things with your business, try new ideas, and create an innovative work culture. As the business leader, you will be responsible for the business environment and culture. Therefore, you have the power and ability to create a business environment and culture that rewards new ways of thinking.

As the business leader, you must lead by example when you have employees. Encourage your employees to think differently. For example, instead of working in the office all day, encourage your employees to work outside in a park or café. Doing so gives your employees more freedom and may even boost their productivity. If it doesn't work out, it's time to try something new. You may even allow your employees to work from home instead of an office if acceptable.

Thinking differently in business doesn't mean reinventing the wheel—rather, it means finding more efficient ways of doing things. Ways that involve happier workers, and not blindly following market trends.

Rule #4: Get the key ingredients

There are two things that make a successful business: an audience and a product or service. When you have a valuable product or service and a large audience, your business will be successful. Take the following people: Will Smith, Taylor Swift, and PewDiePie. What do all of these people have in common? They all have a large audience and a huge fanbase. What else do all of them have in common? It's very easy for them to make money and build a successful business. Will Smith through his movies, Taylor Swift through her music, and PewDiePie through his merchandise.

If you want to be successful working for yourself and have an impactful life purpose, you need to build a large audience and sell your product or service to that audience. This inevitably leads to the question: how do I start building an audience? This is where sales and marketing come into play.

Marketing will help you build an audience, while sales will help you sell to that audience. With the rapid advancement of technology over the past two decades, marketing and sales have never been easier to get into. Online marketing and sales have allowed the average person to do their own marketing and sales from home.

There are some very high-quality books and online course that are taught by professional sales and marketing people with years of experience. To see whether a marketing and sales book is worth reading, check how well-known it is and the amount of copies sold. Because if the author truly knows what they're talking about in sales and marketing, they will have a bestselling book.

If your life purpose includes running your own business, then these two areas will be critical to your success. You can have the best product or service in the world, but if you don't know how to sell it, it will never sell.

Rule #5: Provide overwhelming value

The fifth rule is to provide overwhelming value to people. If you want to be successful in what you do, you must provide your audience with overwhelming value. These days, many businesses try to give out as little value as possible in the hope of later charging the customer when they start asking for more value.

I bet you've searched for a solution to a problem on Google before only to end up on somebody's squeeze page—where if you want to know more or gain the full benefits, you need to purchase their product or service. Only by purchasing the product or service do you get full value.

However, I believe in taking a different approach. I give so much free value that people don't have to think twice about purchasing my other products. I don't do this in a manipulating way though—I do it to show my true value and what I have to offer my audience. An important part of success is giving your audience massive value. What that value is for you I can't tell you—it's something you have to figure out for yourself.

Take Swedish YouTuber PewDiePie for example. He releases daily videos that entertain millions of people. This provides overwhelming value to his audience. So when he asks them to purchase a product or service from him, a huge portion of his fanbase are more than happy to buy it. This is because he places *value* over money.

This is what I encourage you to do as well. Focus on providing overwhelming value to your audience, rather than trying to earn money. If you provide overwhelming value to your audience, money will naturally come as a reward, and you'll love the process of what you do.

Rule #6: Look after yourself

The sixth rule is to look after yourself, as you are the product and the service of your business. When you're doing something you love, it becomes easy to overwork yourself. There is a fine line between hard-working and a workaholic, and it's very easy to step over the line. The difference between the two is how you feel on the inside.

A high performer is someone who works hard when they need to, then rests when they can. A workaholic works hard when they need to and then continues working when they don't need to. When I first started working for myself, I fell into the trap of being a workaholic, and I see a lot of new entrepreneurs fall into the same trap too.

When I started down the road of entrepreneurship, I had a regular work-life balance, working eight hours a day, then resting. But I was also listening to motivational videos and watching YouTube entrepreneur channels, and both of these made me feel I wasn't working hard enough.

Eventually, my 40-hour work week went to 50 hours, as I was convinced I had to work weekends. Then 50 hours turned into 60, and 60 to 70, and before I knew it I was working 90 to 100 hours a week. Even though I was working more hours, my work performance dramatically dropped. I was tired all the time, I felt horrible, and I never allowed myself to have time off.

When we are overworked, we become stressed, which leads to poor nutritional habits, and these eventually lead to poor mental and physical performance. Once that happens, it's easy to develop more negative habits, which will cause you to spiral downwards.

In my personal experience, the reason someone becomes a workaholic is because deep down they feel worthless or incomplete in some way. Of course, this is not the only reason, as there are many factors involved in this problem. But if you find you're overworking yourself and feel guilty for resting, then it's a good place to start making changes.

Make sure you eat a healthy diet, sleep a sufficient amount each night, exercise, and work hard—but not to the point where you become burnt out and stressed. Most importantly, learn how to relax and enjoy your free time, whether it's going to the movies, camping, driving, gaming, dancing, relaxing with friends, or meditation. It can be anything you want—as long as it relaxes you and restores your positive energy to improve your work and life.

Rule #7: Embrace failure and learning

The seventh rule is to continually improve yourself by learning from your failures to be successful as an entrepreneur. Modern society is always changing and adapting, so to stand still is to be left behind. If you stop learning, you stop improving, as you can't have one without the other. It's important that you become a lifelong learner, as that way you will continually improve yourself, and as you do, so will your business. This happens because a business is a reflection of its leader. If the leader of a business doesn't learn and improve, neither will the business.

It's important to understand that failure will come before success. You're going to fail more than you will succeed. As you've probably heard before or experienced personally, failure is much more common than success. It is only by failing and suffering that you experience the most growth.

Of course, when you're going through the pain and suffering of failure, it doesn't feel like it's shaping you. But *it is*. Only by going through the pain of failure will you be strong enough for success. If you were just zapped to the top and achieved success, you wouldn't appreciate it, nor would it satisfy you.

By continually improving yourself, you prevent yourself from getting stuck where you are. When you're trying to achieve something, such as running a successful business, a tricky question arises: how do you know whether you should keep going or give up?

Take for example a business owner who has run a small convenience store for the past decade. The business is mediocre and the owner is struggling to get by. Should he give up or continue running his business in the hope that it will improve?

When you find yourself in such a situation, it can be tough to know what to do next. One solution is for the business owner to learn and improve himself. If he remains the same or gives up, then his dream is lost and with it a decade of hard work. But if he decides to improve himself by reading new business books or taking a marketing course, it will expand his awareness of his situation and enable him to make better decisions in the future. Even if his business fails, then he is better off than he was before he started learning and improving. By continually learning and improving yourself, you will also strengthen your ability to think independently.

You now have seven business rules to get you started in the right direction. In the next chapter, we'll discuss ideology and how to remain independent from it. If you wish to run a business and think independently, understanding how ideology works is important. Because ideology can massively impact business operations, and it also impacts your employee's behaviour and thinking.

Chapter Eleven
Ideology and Remaining Independent

Where there is a supposed truth and the need for acceptance and identity, an ideology will arise. One of the biggest obstacles to independent thinking is ideology, because ideology determines how people think and behave. Ideology is great for influencing the masses, and this is why it's used so much in politics. It helps to determine who is on whose side. In this chapter, we'll look more deeply into ideology and what it means for independent thinking.

What is ideology?

The definition of ideology is "a system of ideas and ideals, especially one which forms the basis of economic or political theory and policy." Think of an ideology as a way for a group of people to think and behave. Take communism and capitalism for example. Both are ideologies that determine how society generally thinks and behaves.

Ideology is an important part of society, because it helps to maintain order and direction. However, because ideology determines how people think and behave, it's easy for corrupt individuals to manipulate other people using ideology. Therefore, a good aim is to follow any ideology you want while simultaneously staying *independent* from it.

It's important to understand that ideology is a tool to shape and improve society, and this tool changes over time. Ideology, like society, changes—and so will people's perspectives about that ideology. Just look at the history of feminism and how much it has changed over time. Or how left-wing and right-wing political parties have adapted and changed over the years.

Whether these changes are good or bad is for you to personally decide. However, it's important to be aware that ideologies change. The next question is why do ideologies change? The answer is: because people and environments change. New experiences, beliefs, ideas, technology, historic events, natural disasters, or famines cause people and ideologies to change.

Ideology plays an important role in many people's lives. Ideology, like dogmatism, becomes a way for people to ground themselves within their reality. This is why some people become very emotional when their ideology is challenged. To challenge their ideology is to challenge their understanding on how society and reality works. This is why ideology is a very political and opinion-heavy topic.

Ideology indoctrination

From my observations on life, I've found there to be three main reasons why people become indoctrinated in ideology. The first is due to their culture, the second is acceptance and identity, and the third is truth.

As humans, we have a strong desire to be accepted by others in some form or another. When someone doesn't feel accepted or that they have a strong identity, they become vulnerable to ideology. The same can be said if they have strong opinions or emotions towards a particular part of society or reality. They become vulnerable, because ideology gives them everything they're looking for: acceptance, identity, and a form of truth.

When an individual is accepted, has an identity, and has a supposed truth, they now feel they have a purpose or something to do with their time and energy. Whether this is their true life purpose depends on the individual and their situation; it's not a yes or no answer. However, this is what religion gives people and why it's so popular. The reason this happens is because humans naturally seek the truth. It's why we gossip, study science, become religious, or follow an ideology. All ideologies offer some form of truth to why something is the way it is, why something is there, or how something got there.

For example, if I were to accept the ideology of capitalism, I would also have a supposed truth in how the economy and society should operate, and it would give me a purpose to spend my time. Which would mostly be defending capitalism against communism and socialism or defending my truth against someone else's truth on how society and reality works. I would now have the identity of a capitalist and be accepted by my fellow capitalists.

The same can be said of veganism, communism, and the list goes on. They all offer a form of acceptance, identity, and truth. This is what grounds us in our understanding of reality. However, every ideology needs to expand, survive, and be different. If you observe an ideology long enough, you will realise that the majority of the ideology's time is spent fighting and defending its basic needs.

Because an ideology is trying to expand, survive, and be different, eventually it will conflict with another ideology. Every ideology has at least one enemy ideology that it disagrees and conflicts with, and the same can be said of religion. For example, Satanism conflicts with Christianity, capitalism conflicts with communism, feminism conflicts with MGTOW, left-wing politics conflicts with right-wing politics, Christian democracy conflicts with conservatism, and so on. As I am sure you've seen hundreds of times, people argue constantly about why their political view is correct or why their ideology is paramount compared to the other.

What's more, every ideology will try to take advantage of its enemy's ideology. Of course, no ideology can ever gain a monopoly over its enemy, but it will sure try. Just ask the capitalist why society would be better without socialism. Or ask the socialist why society would be better without capitalism.

Every ideology and religion loves the idea of holding a monopoly over the world, because it often perceives its truth as the only truth. However, it's impossible for one ideology or religion to hold a monopoly over the world, because everyone has a different perspective on how the world should be. Accordingly, ideologies and religions will always have their enemies, as perspectives will endlessly conflict.

How to deal with ideology or religion

To deal with ideology, I encourage you to be open-minded. This means hearing what other people have to say and understanding their perspective. As you learnt in Chapter 4, if you are offended by what someone else is saying, ask yourself: why is that the case? Instead of reflecting outwardly and telling the other person that they're incorrect, reflect inwardly and understand why they hold such beliefs. Being open-minded doesn't mean you have to agree with what others have to say—just to understand. Nor does it mean blindly accepting beliefs and ideology into your life without question.

When you're part of a group of people who all hold similar beliefs, it's okay to disagree with them. For illustration, if you're feminist, it doesn't mean you have to agree with everything that other feminists say or do. Two people can fight for the same ideology, however it doesn't mean they have to accept and agree with everything their ideology does. Say you belong to a Catholic church, and the church does or supports something you believe is wrong. This doesn't mean you have to blindly follow along with everything they say or do. You have the right to stand up for yourself and hold different opinions.

I believe it's good that people disagree—if it's done in a healthy, non-violent manner. Disagreeing with someone can be a good sign that you're beginning to think for yourself, which is the purpose of this book. Develop a healthy amount of scepticism, but be careful as scepticism can be its own form of ideology. Trust in the small things, however question the big things that greatly impact your life.

When faced with accepting or rejecting an ideology into your life, it's important to think for yourself and not just follow someone else's conclusions. Watch out, because leaders and teachers can be very influential and charming when they're recruiting new members for their group.

To identify areas in your life where you have accepted an ideology, it all comes back to questioning yourself. The key is complete honesty, as without it you're only preventing yourself from growing (remember, no one needs to know these answers but you). In these questions, you can also swap the word "ideology" with "religion" if you like.

Questions: Ideologies

- Why is my ideology correct and the other ideology wrong?
- If my ideology is correct, why do other people believe in something different to me? (Think along the lines of the other person's life experiences.)
- What ideas and beliefs have I been imprinted with?
- Could I be wrong in what I believe?
- What ideas do I love to attack and defend, and why?
- What beliefs and concepts cause me to get emotional?
- What ideas do I identify with?
- Am I only following my ideology because it provides me with acceptance and identity?
- In what ways do I lie to myself?
- Does my ideology fit in with my meaning and purpose in life?
- How would I feel if I had to give up my ideology?
- How does my ideology make the world a better place?
- How does my ideology make the world a worse place?
- What are some common misunderstandings about my ideology?
- In what ways does my ideology use me to spread itself?

I also recommend that you create five other questions to ask yourself to dig deeper into understanding why you believe what you do. It's important to create your own questions, because you know yourself best. Good luck.

Chapter Twelve
Mindfulness and Social Media

Blessed with freewill, and we choose to spend it online! The average person spends two to three hours a day looking at their phone. This doesn't include the number of hours they spend at work and at home on the computer. So in this chapter, we'll look at the impact of social media on our lives and our thinking.

The community of social media

The internet has had a massive impact on society over the past 40 years. With it came social media platforms and apps such as Facebook, Snapchat, Instagram, Reddit, Tinder, YouTube, and Twitter to name a few. Social media is a massive network of people that form an online community. This new online community has become part of our everyday lives. So by having an online account such as Facebook, it means you're part of that community.

Within the community of Facebook, there are sub-communities, such as the pages or groups you like and follow, or your friends list. By following a page like Eminem or Lady Gaga, you become a part of that sub-community. Another way to think of it is that you become a node in a network, which is connected to other nodes.

Be mindful of what you say and do

Because you're part of these sub-communities or networks, it's important to be mindful of what you post online. What you say and post affects other people within that community. This is why what you do online matters, even though it may seem like it doesn't. What you post on social media can change somebody's life for the better or worse.

It's easy to forget that on the other side of a text box or profile picture is a human being with feelings and emotions. Interacting with a screen instead of a person greatly limits our awareness of the other person's emotional reactions and body language. And when our awareness of a situation decreases, we're more likely to do regrettable or harmful things to ourselves and others.

This lack of awareness is what causes people to say and do things online that they wouldn't say or do in real life. Such as telling somebody that their video sucks and that you hate them for it, or that what they believe is stupid, which makes them stupid. Many of these comments are aimed at celebrities or politicians, however it's not uncommon to find groups of people arguing and insulting each other online, and cyberbullying of individuals has massively increased.

With cyberbullying, it's impossible to fully comprehend how a post or comment has affected someone. We may have an idea of the possible effects, but we don't really know, and this can be very dangerous. This is why it's important to be aware that your actions affect other people in ways you don't know the outcome of. Blindly posting negative information and commenting with negative speech creates a negative impact on the people you're connected to, and you don't know the consequences of that action.

What you say and do to a person online matters, just as much as in real life. This means it's important to think and ask yourself: do I really need to post this? It's normal to come across people in life that you don't like or agree with, and this can be even more online. However, hurting that group or person you dislike or disagree with will not fix the problem, nor will it make you feel better. Hurting others only makes the situation worse.

If you want to get through to people, the best way to do that is having a normal conversation with them, without any aggression. The moment the other person senses that you're being aggressive, they will become defensive. And once they become defensive, they will be too busy defending themselves to hear anything you have to say.

It's important to control your actions and emotions here, because if you're not in control of yourself, then somebody else will be. Controlling your emotions doesn't mean ignoring them or neglecting them—rather it means still feeling the emotion but remaining in control. A large part of thinking independently is acting independently, so don't allow other people to control how you feel and respond. It's okay to feel and respond—as long as you're in control of it and not the other person.

Dealing with trolls and negative people online

As you may know, there are people online who spend their time looking for arguments and to troll other people. Often, what these trolls try to do is bait other people with controversial speech or a negative attitude. They want other people to get upset, because that will give them attention and distract them from their personal issues. This is very common in video games, where you may come across people who ruin the game for everyone else so they can get attention and upset everyone else. Or something goes wrong in the game or doesn't go as expected, which causes them to get upset and blame others.

When you encounter a troll or negative person in a game or on social media, it's very easy to fall for the bait and start telling them why they're wrong or begin teasing them back. However, I encourage you not to do this. Just ignore them. If you take the bait and start interacting with them, they will begin to control how you feel and act. Once they control how you feel and act, they start to control your thinking. This happens as you start thinking of ways to get them back or reply to them. Even after your interaction with them is over, it may keep you up at night, as you replay the interaction over and over in your mind.

This is not to say that you can't defend or fight for what you believe is right online, or that you shouldn't get emotional about it. What I am saying is be mindful of the situation and judge whether it's worth your time or not. For example, if somebody is upset that they're losing in a video game and they blame everyone else for it, it's not worth your time to interact with them. Whereas discussing or debating politics with someone online may be worth your time. Whether a situation is worth your time or not is something you must personally decide.

Be mindful of what you read and watch

You now have a good idea why it's important to be mindful of what you say and post. However, it's equally as important to be mindful of what you read and watch, as this can affect you both negatively and positively.

Depending on how the content affects you, this will determine how you think and react. Some content may make you laugh and smile, while other content may make you sad and upset. This is why it's important to be mindful of the type of media you expose yourself to, because it can determine or strongly influence how you think and behave. And remember—if you don't think for yourself, then other people will think for you.

When you're online, it's important not to take everything at face value. For example, it's very common for people to change a story or a headline to make other people have an emotional reaction. Or to quote Donald Trump's favourite words, they create "fake news".

You need to realise that things you read online, such as news stories, aren't necessarily true. A story is just that—a story. When you read a story or a post online, don't just buy into it. Be sceptical of it at first. If the story is something you're interested in and you want to share it, then research it to see whether the other sources match this one.

Fake news is most commonly found in politics, as left-wing and right-wing news stations cover the same topic but produce two different stories from it. This means it's a good idea to get your information from multiple sources. There are some great news websites out there that don't twist and misuse stories for their own political agenda, but it's up to you to sort the wheat from the chaff.

As we covered earlier, the best way to do this is by getting your information from more than one source. This way, you're less likely to be misled and lied to by someone else's conclusions or political agenda. So be mindful of the media you expose yourself to, as what you read and watch influences your thinking.

Questions: Social media and news

- How does what I post and say online affect other people?
- Do I have a positive or negative influence on my online community?
- How does my online influence make me feel?
- How often do I take stories at face value?
- How often do other people control how I feel and act online?
- Is social media having a positive or negative impact on my life?
- In what ways does social media influence the way I think?

When posting online, always be mindful that what you say and do matters, even when it doesn't feel like it. Just because a person doesn't interact with a post (such as liking it or sharing it), this doesn't mean it didn't have an effect on them. Thinking independently involves being mindful of how you impact others, because you're part of a network. This means the way other people think within your network influences the way you think. Therefore, be mindful of your online influence and always think before you post.

Chapter Thirteen
Investing in Yourself

To not invest in the present is to have a poor future. It's important to invest in yourself and not waste your time. In fact, your time is the most valuable resource that you have. The way you spend your time determines and influences the way you think. In this chapter, we'll look at the value of time and using it to invest in yourself.

The value of time

There are two reasons why time is the most valuable resource you have. The first reason is because your time is limited and is continually running out. The second reason is because you don't know how much time you have left. Your time is a limited resource. You don't know how much you have left of it, and it's continually getting smaller and smaller.

When you're young, it's easy to forget the value of your time, as it can feel that your youth will stay around forever. This was something I often did in my teenage years. When I was fifteen, I would justify wasting my time by saying "In ten years' time, I'll be twenty-five, so I've got heaps of time". I didn't realise just how valuable my time was.

With the rapid advancement of technology, the world is becoming full of things that distract us and waste our time.

New movies, new video games, new social media apps, not to mention an endless supply of YouTube videos. With all of these distractions, it can be very easy to waste your time, especially when you're young. Because who wants to face responsibilities and hard work when the alternative is no responsibilities and little to no work?

However, your attention is your power, so when you get distracted wasting time on social media or watching pointless YouTube videos, these distractions take away your power and your time. That's why it's important to be mindful of how you spend your time.

Be mindful with money

It's also important to be aware of what you're spending your money on. How you spend your money greatly impacts how you think, and very few people realise this. Say you win $100. There are two ways you can spend it. The first way is to spend it on junk food, a new video game, new clothes, clubbing, or some other form of entertainment. The second way is by spending it on a book, an online course, a documentary, investing the money for the future, buying healthy food, or some other form of benefitable product or service. What do you spend it on?

There are two ways that people use money. The first is wasting money on something that doesn't benefit them. The second is spending money on something that benefits you or another person. You'd be surprised by how many people waste their money on products and services that leave them worse off than they were before.

It's okay to spend money on relaxation and entertainment—as long as it doesn't become excessive. For example, it's fine to play a video game as a form of relaxation after a hard day of work, as this would be considered a benefit. However, the video game may become a problem if it's causing you to spend hundreds of dollars for in-game items, which would be wasting your money. Whether a product or service is benefitable or not completely depends on your personal situation. Accordingly, use your own judgement in deciding whether a product or service is a waste of your time or not.

It's important to organize your environments by separating work from entertainment. For example, you may have a small area in your house that is for work and study, whereas the bedroom is for relaxation and entertainment. By separating the two environments, you greatly reduce the chances of you becoming distracted and wasting your time.

Your daily environment influences how you think and act. So, when you purchase time-wasting products or services and put them in an environment that you're supposed to be productive in, they begin to negatively influence how you think and behave. Instead of studying and working when you're supposed to, you get distracted and waste your time by being unproductive. Being mindful of your environment and the distractions within it can go a long way to increasing your productivity and independent thinking.

Another important factor in independent thinking is controlling the types of environments you expose yourself to. The environments you choose to spend your time in determine the outlook of your future. This is because we become what we think about. This is a simple concept, but very true.

What you think about all day long determines what you manifest in your future. If you think in positive terms, you will manifest positive results within your life. However, if you think in negative terms, you will manifest negative results. If you think and believe in running your own charity, you will find that your goals in life will naturally manifest the results you want. Whereas, if you think and believe in becoming nothing, then those are the results you will manifest within your life.

For this reason, it's important to be mindful of how you think. Of course, becoming what you think has a practical, logical side to it. You can't think of having superpowers and expect to wake up the next morning being able to shoot webs out of your palms like Spiderman. However, you can expect to create the life that you want with the right mindset.

Procrastination

Another way we waste time is by avoiding things we know we need to do. Instead of doing what we need to do, we procrastinate and spend our time doing things we know we shouldn't be doing. The main reason we procrastination is because we're stressed. When you procrastinate doing an assignment, report, or activity, it's because you're stressed. This stress can come from the fear of failure, anxiety, or even lack of sleep. The longer you procrastinate on a task, the worse the stress becomes. However, being disciplined can help you deal with procrastination. This begs the question: how can I be more disciplined?

In today's modern world, it can feel like we're not truly free because we're restricted by jobs, money, debts, fears, and other physical limitations. As we live in such conditions, it's easy for our minds to wander and think about how great life would be if only we had true freedom or more freedom than we currently have; that way, we could do as we please. However, what you must realise is that with freedom comes responsibility. If you have freedom but don't take the responsibility to discipline yourself, nothing fruitful will come from that freedom.

A lot of people experience times where they don't feel free in life; instead they feel stuck and trapped. This is where discipline and responsibility come into play. When you have responsibilities in your life that need to be fulfilled, it requires discipline to handle those responsibilities correctly. Without discipline, you will either procrastinate with your responsibilities or do a poor job.

Discipline sometimes means doing things we don't feel like doing. For example, most days when I walk into the gym, I don't feel like working out. I could easily come up with 101 excuses for not working out today. But because working out and looking after myself is my own responsibility, it's important that I remain disciplined. If I'm not disciplined and avoid the responsibility of looking after my own health, I will suffer the negative consequences of my actions. Notice how I am free to choose to look after myself, and how looking after myself requires responsibility and discipline.

Accordingly, discipline involves you facing the things you don't feel like doing. The one trait that every successful person has in their life is discipline, from athletes to actors, singers to CEOs, presidents to prime ministers. They all require discipline. Discipline is not a prison—in fact, discipline is your ticket to freedom.

It's not uncommon to associate discipline with living a boring and restrictive life. However, this is far from the truth. If you have discipline, you will have more freedom in your life than those who are not disciplined. If you're disciplined with your money, you will have more financial freedom compared those who are not disciplined with their money. For illustration, the disciplined person invests and saves their money for the future. The undisciplined person spends their money as soon as they get it and doesn't save for the future.

If you're disciplined with your body, you will have more freedom compared to those who are not disciplined with their body. For example, if you discipline yourself to practice calisthenics on a weekly basis, your body will be stronger and fitter compared to someone who doesn't practice calisthenics. Because you're disciplined with your body, it gives you more freedom, such as being up to do 20 pullups in a row, run up a mountain, or go rock climbing. If you don't discipline your body and neglect your health, you wouldn't have the fitness to do these things.

To be more disciplined, you must take responsibility for yourself and create order in your life. For example, setting up a schedule and developing good habits, which we discussed in earlier chapters. If you wish to have more freedom within your life, you must take the responsibility upon yourself to be more disciplined. Because to neglect responsibility and to continually procrastinate will end in you not getting the life you want.

Questions: Time

- In what ways do I waste my time?
- How much time do I waste in a day?
- How am I undisciplined?
- Why am I undisciplined?
- What do I think about the most?
- Do I benefit from the way I currently think, if not how can I change it?
- Do I spend my money on products or services that increase my wellbeing?
- In what ways does my environment distract me?

How to Think Independently

Your time is the most valuable asset you have, so it's important not to waste it. To not waste your time involves being disciplined and taking responsibility for yourself. You may have more questions on how exactly you can discipline your mind when it seems to be all over the place. In the next chapter, we will discuss mediation, which is a practical exercise you can use to become more disciplined and less distracted by your own mind.

Chapter Fourteen
The Importance of Meditation

A peaceful mind is a productive mind. Meditation is a powerful tool that can be used to strengthen your mind and improve your overall wellbeing. For this entire book, I have been asking you to reflect inwardly and question yourself. Meditation is something that complements this inward reflection perfectly, as both of these cause you to be more aware and conscious of yourself. In this chapter, I'll talk about the benefits of meditation, then show you how to meditate.

What is meditation?

When most people think of meditation, they picture a monk meditating for hours and hours or perceive it as some religious thing. Consequently, most people quickly dismiss it as something useless or hippy woo woo. However, I would like to encourage you to be open-minded and start a meditation habit.

Note, you don't have to be religious to mediate. If you are religious, such as being Catholic or Muslim, then meditation is not a sin or against God. In fact, I have met many religious people who claim that mediation has helped them get closer to their God.

The benefits of meditation

There are many benefits of meditation, and these are just some of them:
- Reduces stress
- Makes you happier
- Helps you manage anxiety and depression
- Improves sleep
- Improves pain tolerance
- Improves your memory
- Improves self-awareness and general awareness
- Improves concentration
- Decreases blood pressure
- Improves discipline
- Improves patience
- Improves emotional control
- Improve emotional intelligence
- Improves information-processing and decision-making
- Improves relaxation

As you can see, there are many benefits to be gained from meditating. In fact, many of these improve your ability to think independently, such as improved sleep, memory, self-awareness, concentration, emotional intelligence, information-processing, and decision-making.

How to mediate

Now you have a good understanding of some of the benefits of mediation, let's look at how you can mediate, even if you've never done it before. There are multiple ways to meditate, and because of this, it can be confusing whether you're meditating correctly or not. Fear not, as I will give you three simple meditation techniques to get you started. After you've mastered these three, feel free to explore other types of meditation that you feel will benefit you the most.

Mindfulness meditation

The first form of meditation is mindfulness meditation. Throughout the book, you've probably noticed me using the word "mindful", which means "to be more conscious and aware of something".

Mindfulness meditation involves observing your own thoughts as they drift through your mind. The purpose of this meditation is not to get involved with the thoughts—rather to observe what they do. Observing your thoughts can help you identify your patterns of thinking. Knowing the nature of your thoughts is paramount when it comes to thinking independently. And being aware of your thoughts will greatly improve your ability to think independently.

To begin mindfulness meditation, simply follow these steps:
1. Sit or lie down in a comfortable position, in a quiet, non-distracting environment. This can be your bedroom, lounge, or even outside in the garden. Anywhere that you find peaceful and relaxing.

2. Close your eyes and begin to observe your thoughts. Pay attention to what they say, where they go, where they come from, and how they make you feel.
3. Observe your thoughts for the next 15 to 60 minutes.

Whenever you get dragged into the thought and forget that you are supposed to be observing the thought, simply bring yourself back to the present moment and begin observing your thoughts again.

When you're just beginning to practice mindfulness meditation, you will constantly find yourself getting lost in your thoughts. This is perfectly normal, and it's important not to get frustrated with yourself when it happens.

If this is your first-time practicing meditation, I recommend just meditating for 15 minutes a day. All you need to do is carve out 15 minutes a day to meditate. It can be in the morning or at night—that's for you to decide.

Over time, you can slowly increase this until you're meditating for 60 minutes or more. How long you should meditate for is completely up to you—meditate for as long as you feel you need to. However, the long-term goal is to slowly increase the amount of time you meditate every day.

Concentration meditation

The second form of meditation is concentration meditation. Concentration meditation involves focusing on a single point. This can be anything such as a book, a cup, your hand, a chair, a pillow, a candle flame, the wall, or even your breath. The point of this meditation is to practice focusing on a single point for as long as you can.

To begin concentration meditation, simply follow these steps:

1. Find an object or something to focus on.
2. Once you've found something to focus on, sit down and begin focusing and observing the object for the next 15 to 60 minutes.

As you sit down and focus on the object, you will notice your mind start to drift away. Once you're aware that your mind has drifted away, simply bring it back to the present moment and focus on the object again. Concentration meditation will help improve your awareness and concentration.

Breathing meditation

The third form of meditation is breathing mediation. Breathing meditation involves focusing on your breath and breathing in and out deeply. This form of meditation is great for relaxation and helps reduce stress and anxiety.

To being breathing meditation, simply follow these steps:

1. Sit or lie down in a comfortable position, in a quiet, non-distracting environment.
2. Close your eyes and bring your focus to your breath.
3. Begin to breath in and out deeply and slowly. Breathe in and then back out for as long you need. Make sure your breathing feels comfortable and natural.
4. Continue to focus on your breath for the next 15 to 60 minutes.

As you focus on your breathing, you will notice your mind starting to drift away. If this happens, simply bring your mind back to the present moment and focus on your breathing again.

You now have three simple meditation techniques to try. A common theme you may have noticed is that your mind will keep drifting away. This is commonly known as "monkey mind". If you implement a meditation habit, you will notice that your monkey mind never sits still and will take you away from the present moment. The more you meditate, the less your monkey mind will bother you. This will allow you to be in the present moment with improved focus and concentration.

I strongly encourage you to meditate, as it will teach you a lot about yourself and the nature of your own mind. This will greatly increase your ability to think independently, because it's one thing to know yourself—and it's another thing to know your own mind.

Conclusion

Congratulations on making it to the end of the book, as not everybody has made it this far. The knowledge and skills you've acquired in this book have put you at an advantage compared to most people.

You now know yourself at a very deep level, and you may be surprised at the amount of people who don't know themselves as well as you now know yourself. As you've seen, the key to knowing anything in life is **questioning**. The reason why so many people don't know who they are in life is because they have never questioned themselves. However, you have a deeper understanding compared to those who refuse to question themselves.

You now understand that thinking independently is all about questioning yourself and reflecting inwardly. The power of thinking independently has enabled you to find meaning in life and create your own life purpose. You've seen that finding a meaning in life and creating your own life purpose comes from within. Remember, whenever you feel lost, simply reflect inwardly and question. Every answer you have about yourself can be found within.

Now you have the ability to research any topic or idea you want, without relying on the traditional education system to do it. You have a deeper understanding of social media, society, and ideology, which is very important as they all impact the way you think and behave. With your understanding, you can now safely interact with social media, society, and ideology without worrying about them negatively influencing you. This is important because society and ideology can be very deep and complex topics.

Accordingly, if you wish to have a better understanding of society, ideology, human behaviours, worldviews, and values, then I highly recommend researching spiral dynamics, which builds on the research of professor Clare W. Graves. Spiral dynamics is a powerful model that enables you to better understand different worldviews and values, including your own. It does this by presenting eight stages that allow you to understand and perceive different levels of worldviews and values in detail. In fact, it's a model I use to guide myself on my personal journey of thinking independently. It is also a model I refer to when writing about society and ideology.

In addition, feel free to check out my website www.glennbaloban.com, which has free additional resources to further improve your ability to think independently. There, you can also find my online course and other books. You can also contact me through the site, so feel free to ask me any questions you might have.

My next book will be about the nature of existence, where I will discuss the formlessness of existence among other topics such as where thoughts come from and how our imagination works. So, be sure to stay updated for my next book as I will share ideas and theories never discussed before. Anyway, that is enough of my self-promoting.

Going forward, I encourage you to use the power of thinking independently to make the world a better place. To keep your mind independent, you must always be questioning. Question society, your teachers, and most importantly question yourself. Because the moment you stop questioning is the moment that dogmatism begins to grow, blossoming into limiting beliefs. Finding the answers to life's questions within yourself ensures that you remain independent.

I have taught you everything you need to know to begin your journey to independence, and you now have the ability and skill set to continue on your own. Independence is there if you want it—you just need to take action. It's now time for you to begin your journey and start thinking independently.

Good luck.

Glossary

Conditioning is a learning process where someone's behaviour is changed due to being rewarded or punished each time they do or don't perform a certain action

Dogmatism means believing that ideas or principles are facts, despite them being based on unproven assumptions rather than evidence. Also, being narrow-minded, lacking tolerance, or being inflexible in your views.

Enlightenment means having advanced information or knowledge, especially of the spiritual kind; being freed from ignorance and misinformation; being in a state of awakened understanding.

Indoctrinated means being instructed in a paradigm or ideology, especially dogmatically, or brainwashed."

Nihilism is the denial or lack of belief in the meaningful aspects of life or in the intrinsic value of life itself.

Paradigm a paradigm is a typical or stereotypical example, pattern, or model of behaviour. A set of assumptions, concepts, values and practices that create a way of viewing reality for the community that share them.

About the Author

Glenn Baloban is an INTJ, who is on a lifelong mission to make the world a more conscious and better place.

For any questions about the book or to speak to Glenn, please contact him at www.glennbaloban.com.

Author image by Jacinta Eve.

www.ingramcontent.com/pod-product-compliance
Lightning Source LLC
LaVergne TN
LVHW041645060526
838200LV00040B/1724